Practical Aspects of Outreach

Practical Aspects

of

Outreach

David L. Martin

Rod and Staff Publishers, Inc.
P.O. Box 3, Hwy. 172
Crockett, KY 41413
Telephone: (606) 522-4348

Copyright 2006
by Rod and Staff Publishers, Inc.
Crockett, KY 41413

Printed in U.S.A.

ISBN 0-7399-2367-6
Catalog no. 2368

1 2 3 4 5 — 15 14 13 12 11 10 09 08 07 06

Contents

Foreword **9**
1. Where It All Begins **11**
2. Catching the Vision **15**
    Discerning the Call 15
    Choosing Personnel 20
    The Decision to Go or Stay 28
3. First Decisions on the Field **35**
    Money 35
    Housing 43
    A Sanctuary 45
    Jobs and Businesses 51
    School 51
    Local Laws 59
4. Reaching the Community **67**
    Efforts by the Church 67
    Personal Contacts 97
5. Taking a Stand on Issues **109**
    Upholding the Standards 109
    Relating to Other Church Groups 114
    Divorce and Remarriage 115
    Other Issues 117
6. Life at Home **121**
    Family Life and Outreach Work 121
    Company 122
    Tips for Visitors 123
    Foster Children 126
    Homes for Young Adults 130
7. Life in the Congregation **133**
    Keeping Ties With the Home Church 133
    Relationships Within the Local Brotherhood 136

Our Attitude Toward Incoming Mennonites	142
Culture Shock	149
The Needs of New Members	154
New Members With Special Difficulties	157
8. Some Thoughts in Closing	**169**
Losses	169
Growth	176
Rewards	179

Foreword

"And of some have compassion, making a difference: and others save with fear, pulling them out of the fire."

Jude 22, 23

It is an old complaint and a true one: "Sometimes the book will tell you everything but what you need to know." Unfortunately, this will have to be another one of those books. People's needs vary so much, and some are so sensitive that cold print might not do justice to their situation. It takes private discussion with each other and with the Lord to work out some of these things.

Further, the suggestions this book does venture to make are not all absolute. Some people involved in outreach "do it all wrong" and still make out nicely or at least muddle their way through and find the grace of God sufficient. In fact, sometimes God uses the less-than-ideal to serve purposes of His own and to bring great glory to His Name.

Yet, some principles and illustrations found here should be helpful to people who start a new outreach, as well as to those who support them. Most important, in the end it should be a blessing to those priceless individuals to whom we are reaching out.

Practical Aspects of Outreach is about home missions, but here and there you will find illustrations drawn from foreign missions. No doubt foreign missionaries can benefit from some of the things said here.

The writer of this book, David L. Martin, acknowledges the help of many friends who contributed much from their wide variety of experiences and store of enthusiasm.

Chapter 1

Where It All Begins

> *"And the Ancient of days did sit, whose garment was white as snow, and the hair of his head like the pure wool. . . . A fiery stream issued and came forth from before him: thousand thousands ministered unto him, and ten thousand times ten thousand stood before him."*
>
> *Daniel 7:9, 10*

"Begin at the beginning" is always good advice. Never is it better than in the matter of reaching out to people. No wonder the Bible starts out with "In the beginning God . . ." For the Bible is God's great attempt to reach out to people. God begins with Himself. He expects His outreach workers to begin there too.

God is the great power source for His outreach efforts. Before we start considering the practicalities of outreach work, we have to understand this. Practical considerations are fine, but without God they become meaningless.

Even the more directly spiritual efforts can leave God a little off to the side if we are not careful. We can strive to bring conviction into people's hearts, forgetting that only God can do this through Jesus Christ and His Spirit. We can give good counsel, but finally only God can bless our efforts. We cannot bless them ourselves.

God has His ways of teaching us this lesson. In one brother's

Chapter 1

opinion, there has been more success with the people God brought to us than with the people we have worked hard to help. Maybe you have noticed too that, while we look in one direction for success, it slips into our lives from another. The point is simple. *God* does it. *He* gives the increase.

How shall we respond to all this? Shall we not work hard? Of course, but we should make sure that a fair amount of our hard work goes into our relationship with the Lord. We need to spend time communicating with God, reading His message to us, and maintaining fellowship with Him in prayer.

Missionaries whom God has used have all spent a healthy portion of their time in communion with God. Some of them have organized round-the-clock prayer chains. Some have fasted at length. Even if we do not copy all their methods, we do well to catch their spirit.

Finally, God wants not so much to be our avenue to success as He wants for our successes (and failures) to be our avenue to Him. All our efforts to bring others to the Lord not only should do just that but also should bring us closer to the Lord. We must not only begin at the beginning but also end at the end.

People are a beginning consideration too. People are people—not souls in the abstract, but individuals with personalities. Each has his set of memories, regrets, ideals, fears, and hopes. If we knew them to the depths of their being, we would love them, much as God does.

People not only have personalities but also possibilities. "A stranger is a friend you have not met yet." We have found this true countless times. People we knew vaguely or not at all ten years ago have moved into our lives, and now we could hardly do without them. It is mildly exciting to meet people and wonder how we might view them ten years from now.

This is especially interesting when we think that sinners are saints we have not won yet. One brother was heard to say, as

Where It All Begins

he saw a man standing along the street, "That might be the next convert in our church. I will go and talk to him."

Of course, when we view people, we must look beyond even this. Let us try to glimpse what the Lord has in mind for them in the great moment of truth that the apostle Paul described so well. "For what is our hope, or joy, or crown of rejoicing? Are not even ye in the presence of our Lord Jesus Christ at his coming?" (1 Thessalonians 2:19).

People are what outreach is all about, and we must make them a priority. Someone came to a brother serving an outreach and said, "How would it be if I took your boys with my boys for an outing on Saturday? We could do some hiking and things like that . . ." The brother's first impulse was, *I need the boys myself that day.* Then he thought, *But people are why we are here! And this is one who has proven himself trustworthy.* He sent the boys, and the Lord blessed his day.

People sense whether we value them. Someone described outreach workers he knew as "welcoming without including . . . offering without sharing." Maybe he was overly critical. Still, much more positive is the story of a minister who called acquaintances to see how they were getting along. The lady's reaction was, "Oh, Mr. Gehman! I'm so glad someone cares!"

Eternity. As a young man, Ivins Steinhauer came into the church and later became an effective and memorable preacher. In one of his sermon illustrations, he told about a time he attended a Mennonite worship service. A member approached him afterwards and asked, "What were your impressions of the service?"

Ivins replied, "I've been wondering about the little sign you have under the clock on the wall. It says, 'eighty-six a minute.' What does that mean?"

The brother replied, "That means every minute eighty-six people die and go to a Christless grave, a lost eternity."

That was years ago. The figure would be different today,

Chapter 1

but the solemnity of that fact remains. Every one of the people we meet is headed either for fadeless glory or for eternal horror and despair. God does not ask us to reach them all, but He wants very much for us to reach some.

CHAPTER 2

Catching the Vision

Discerning the Call

"As they ministered to the Lord, and fasted, the Holy Ghost said . . ."

Acts 13:2

How can you tell if God is calling your congregation or fellowship to expand into a new area?

First, one person does not decide this all by himself. The vision might begin with one person, but then the church leaders must be involved, and finally the whole congregation or fellowship. Even if not everyone helps to make the final decision, all should know what is happening and feel free to share their ideas.

A need is not always a call. Thousands of locations, especially in foreign countries, have crying needs. Practically anywhere we go with the Gospel, people will respond. Perhaps this means we should go more places than we are going. But it does not mean we should go just anywhere. We cannot do everything. All we can do is go where the Lord leads us.

Watch two main indicators: the kind of need in the new area and the resources at home.

The picture at home. Could the home congregation function if it gave several families away? Or could several congregations working together each supply a family for a new work?

Are you considering expanding your home church building

to accommodate all the people? There could be good reasons for expanding the building, but God blesses congregations who put forth the effort to expand their outreach instead.

Are there people at home with an interest in reaching out? Are they lovers of other people? If not, maybe the work must first begin at home, kindling a fire! But if the fire is already there, that could be God's call.

The picture on the field. Is there interest in what you represent, or would there be with a little encouragement? Maybe you want to hold public meetings, advertise for them, and see who shows up. Maybe you want to have Bible studies in homes for a while to measure the local interest.

Has another church invited you to the area? Maybe the people of that church see many needs around them but do not have the resources to answer all the calls. Maybe they want a broader and more stable fellowship than they presently have. Naturally, one must be careful about moving into a sensitive situation and trying to solve long-standing problems.

Are there people to whom you have a responsibility? One congregation began when a woman came from Texas to join a church in Georgia. Her husband remained in Texas. The church encouraged her to go back and live with her husband—but then they had the problem of knowing how to supply fellowship to their distant member. They visited Texas and worshiped there every six weeks, eventually establishing a resident congregation.

Remain aware that the people who attract a church into an area may not continue with that church. "We be good Mennonites," said a Russian man newly in the States, encouraging friends to establish a church in his community. Later he seemed taken aback to find out he would not be considered one of the leaders. Perhaps for this or other reasons, he led his family away to a different setting.

However, the fear that the first interest will die away is

Catching the Vision

hardly a good enough reason to refuse to start an outreach. By the time the first Macedonian call no longer seems clear, the church usually has found other reasons to stay with the work. More people from the locality have become interested, and the enterprise goes on.

How some churches started. One outreach began after a Christian farmer peddled produce across the mountain from his home and saw the spiritual poverty there. He was especially concerned about the many children growing up without spiritual training. After the brother shared his concern, the church moved forward with the work.

Another congregation began with a discussion among three brethren in a field. They thought a conservative church should be established near Gap, Pennsylvania. A year later they started meeting in a home.

Another congregation began when two families withdrew from their respective congregations because of deterioration in church standards there. With nowhere else to turn, they worshiped together in each other's homes until they could build a church.

Church began at Tamaqua, Pennsylvania, after explorers had been investigating the Wilkes-Barre–Scranton area. "On one occasion, on the way home from Scranton, they had gotten on the wrong street in Tamaqua and had driven into the South Ward section of town. From our perspective today, it is apparent that this was God's way of opening the door to a work in Tamaqua. Later, one of the brethren who was helping to investigate farther north said, 'It seems as though we are running into a stone wall. Let's try Tamaqua.' "[1]

The church at Vanderhoof, British Columbia, began after

---

[1] James Martin and Kenneth Mast, "The History of the New England Valley Mennonite Church," *The Eastern Mennonite Testimony,* January 1996, p. 5.

CHAPTER 2

Mennonites had driven through it for several years on their way to Decker Lake and Danskin. When several families from Vanderhoof showed interest, it became apparent that Vanderhoof might be a fertile field. It was.

The Danskin, British Columbia, congregation began when Mervin Baer from McBride shared a hospital room with Henry Amendt from Danskin. They got to talking, and Mervin discovered that Henry had already established a Mennonite congregation in his community and wanted better leadership than himself. The McBride church provided this for a time and then turned leadership over to another church fellowship.

The Highland congregation in Delaware began from the Wilmington VS unit. When the VS men had completed their service, some of them felt called to stay in the area and help the new congregation. Eventually the VS unit closed, but by then the congregation was established.

The church at Loma, Colorado, started due to a seeking family that wanted fellowship. Church friends from Farmington, New Mexico, visited with them over a period of four or five years. Later they had monthly services with them and rented a house for visiting families to live in during weekends. They also used it as a place of worship. Eventually they started a church, choosing two ministers and four other families to move there.

A church began near Cheyenne, Wyoming, after three Christian women were longing and praying for a more consistent church fellowship. One of them was homeschooling her family. Through using Rod and Staff school material, she began to ask questions about our faith and practice. The publishing house referred this contact to the Northwest Fellowship churches to visit and research the interest. Since these ladies could not easily move to an established congregation, several families moved to the area to provide fellowship for them.

Catching the Vision

A church that did not start. Sometimes a need is apparent, but the church does not move ahead for practical reasons, as is shown in the following report from Guatemala.

> While the bishop brethren were here, we had a service at Chuicabal, a small village approximately a twenty-minute drive from Edén where new interest is being shown. The call is coming for us to begin a church there as there is no evangelical church in the area. There were between twenty-five and thirty persons from the neighborhood at the service which was held in Don Arturo's house. This is a man who has been walking an hour and a half to our Sunday morning services in Edén. Because of a lack of personnel, we have decided not to establish a church there at this time. We will have services there one Sunday afternoon a month, encouraging them to walk to Edén the other Sundays.[2]

Poor reasons for starting a work. It looks like fun. There is nothing wrong with a sense of adventure; it even helps to energize people for a while. However, a sense of adventure grows thin when a new work grows a little older, so there must be more that energizes people than just that.

Secondly, several families may have gotten their heads together and decided to move to a new area for personal reasons. If the church does not lead the way, there has probably already been trouble, and more is coming.

Sometimes consideration of a move is made too lightly. A congregation looks around and sees that other congregations are starting new works here and there. Why not they too? But they miss the serious seeking after the Lord that should attend

---

[2] The Leland Seibel family, "Guatemala News: Letter From the Field," *The Eastern Mennonite Testimony,* February 1988, p. 12.

CHAPTER 2

such a move, and in the end they miss the ingathering of souls they might have had with more sensitivity to His leading.

Financial attractions, such as cheap land, have strong appeal, but they are not a basis on which to build a soul-winning venture. It may mean that people who are more interested in dollars than anything else are likely to flood in from home churches.

Finally, threats to the spiritual life of our families are a crucial matter. During the 1870s, many Mennonites left Russia because the government had threatened to remove their exemption from military service. The government backed down, but the ones who left made out much better in the long run than those who stayed.

Choosing Personnel

"Lay hands suddenly on no man."

1 Timothy 5:22

Suitable candidates. Look for people appreciated at home. If no one needs them there, why should the mission field want them? Find people who are already busy serving the Lord and reaching out to help others.

Of course, some people are so much needed at home that they cannot realistically pull themselves away. When a church sends its "cream of the crop" too often, it may soon have problems at home. So the question is, Can a person release himself from his home responsibilities, or can he not? Can he do it over time?

Look for people who can blend in with the group. A person's traits will stand out more at a small church, where there are only half a dozen families. Maybe you want to leave certain brethren back home where a larger church fellowship can absorb some of their "strong points."

Look for flexible people, persons willing to bend with circumstances and adapt to sudden changes. Part of starting a new outreach involves exploring blind alleys and backing out of them. "We will have our worship services here. . . . No, that's not a good idea after all." "The Miller family will rent the house on the hill. . . . No, the Yoder family will buy it instead." Personnel must know how to call this kind of thing business as usual, and smile.

Find a variety of people, some older and some younger. Have several families with children and youth so that people from the community, no matter what age they are, can find someone with whom to relate.

The largeness of a family can be both an asset and a liability. If a family is large, it may be difficult to find a house of sufficient size. On the other hand, they add a positive social dimension much appreciated by the children in the area.

Look for families who are stable enough to endure some rough times. Someone guessed that a family who moves can expect to lose a year's income. Certainly, it should come as no surprise if a family does.

Look for families you know, families with a good record. They should not be the disgruntled from some congregation you know little about. They might want to come to your outreach in order to make it what *they* want it to be. It may be right to say no to people who want to take part. That could be easier than solving difficulties they create in the end.

There may be a place for asking someone to serve for a short time just to help get the work going. A retired businessman could be just the one. He might develop a lasting interest in the work and contribute advice long after he has moved back home.

Ideal size for the original group. Six is not necessarily the perfect number of families, but it is a good one. If you have fewer, then sometimes the superintendent and his wife will both be teaching Sunday school classes and the preacher will be doing some of the song leading. Certainly, it can be done,

CHAPTER 2

but it is awkward. Stories about the Sunday school teacher losing half of his audience when his wife steps out are amusing to tell but should describe only temporary situations.

More important than this, however, is that one or two families alone do not create enough of a spiritual presence in the congregation. They do not create enough appearance of stability to make membership attractive. If a number of families from the community come, the congregation is liable to end up simply being a community church without adequate influence to build solidly. For instance, in one congregation, two families were members; other families attended because it was a nice place to go. But they seemed to sense little obligation to make a commitment to the church.

At another congregation, the same problem surfaced in a different form. In this instance, many people did become members despite the minimal presence of outreach personnel in the congregation. They thought very highly of the brother and his family who had conservative background. In the words of one observer, "They thought he could walk on water." However, the very fact that he was held up so high exposed his flaws too. This reduced his effectiveness.

If too few families come from a conservative background, the congregation might develop a mentality of its own. This might not be obvious at first, but it can become evident when children from the new families grow up and begin testing church boundaries.

So much for having a large enough beginning group. On the other hand, do not make the beginning group so big that visitors from the community feel overwhelmed when they walk in the door. Of course, we hope the church will grow and in a sense create this problem by its own prosperity. But we should not create it ahead of time. Neither do we want the general community to feel threatened by a sudden major influx of strangers.

Catching the Vision

Look for families like-minded to each other. In some ways it would be ideal to have them all come from the same congregation. This is often not practical, of course. Moreover, we all know that we can sometimes be more like-minded with a friend from a thousand miles away than with someone much nearer. The point is that we choose people who can work together with as many details agreed upon beforehand as possible. No doubt all of us have met individuals who left us somewhat bewildered because their reasoning processes were so different from ours. And some of us have proceeded "as normal" only to discover that certain new friends were shocked at our misbehavior! We want to avoid this at an outreach.

It may be helpful if the nucleus of families has a chance to get settled and acquainted with each other for at least a year before more new families move in. The sending church might even stipulate this.

Sample questionnaire. When one church considered starting a new work, each head of home received a paper giving some information and asking questions like the following:

> We ask you to prayerfully consider and answer the following questions:
>
> 1. Are you agreed to proceed with the work of starting a congregation at Jonesville?
>
> 2. We as a ministry feel that we should provide two ordained brethren in leadership right at the beginning of the work, with at least one of them being experienced in the ministry. Which two of the local ministry would you nominate to go with their families to Jonesville?
>
> 3. Do <u>you</u> sense any leading from the Lord to move to Jonesville?
>
> 4. Would there be hindrances to your moving, especially financial hindrances such as debts, present commitments, or obligations? Please explain.

CHAPTER 2

    5. Would you consider moving if you were asked by the church?
    6. Would you like to nominate other families to move? List them.

Finding leaders for the field is a critical decision for the same reason it is critical back home. A leader may not be more important or hardworking than anyone else, but he serves as a point of reference for what goes on. People call him to say, "I wonder what you think of this idea" even if they know of no reason why it would not be good. Just getting his stamp of approval reassures them. Knowing that the outreach has a leader improves the comfort level of the group.

When choosing a leader, remember that what he does not do can be as important as what he does do. If he is the kind who succeeds by not failing, he might be your man. A quiet brother might do a good job once the responsibility falls on him.

Ideally, the outreach should have more than one ordained leader. Since leaders have different personalities and varying gifts, members may feel more free relating more closely with one than with the other. Sometimes a leader makes a mistake, and the members involved do not feel free to confront him on the matter. So they share it with the other leader, who has the first leader's confidence, and the two can discuss and work it out together. Then too a leader with one kind of personality might be able to touch people that the other leader cannot, and vice versa. This is part of normal church life. Of course, if people start saying, "I am of Paul" and "I am of Apollos" (1 Corinthians 3:4), or if the brethren in the ministry start seeing each other as rivals, then the concept has gone too far.

Leaders who come to an outreach should already be acquainted with each other and have shown that they can work together. They must be similar in conviction. Churches sometimes suffer because of difficulties among the ministry,

Catching the Vision

and members newly coming into the church are especially vulnerable in these cases.

Leaders are hard to find because they are already so busy. So then why not simply ordain a man for the work and send him promptly to the outreach? This has actually been done, and the results have not been altogether bad. But most people agree that this method is not the best. Inexperience is just what we do not need. It is better to send leaders who have already been leaders. Then the home church can ordain men to fill the vacancy left by the experienced leaders who have departed for the outreach.

The above arrangement does at least solve the problem of having a series of short-term leaders, which no one likes. About the time the congregation warms up to one man and his family, he is gone and another takes his place. This especially frustrates people who are still trying to find their way into the congregation and who are perhaps even wondering whether this church is the place for them.

The problem takes on an added twist when a minister would like to extend his term on the field but finds himself recalled by his home congregation. Not only does this cause discomfort on the outreach end, but it also is not altogether good for the image of the home congregation. To avoid this, the minister and his congregation should have a clear understanding of each other's expectations from the beginning. At least they should try!

Administrative questions. How do you direct the new work? At one new work, a committee directed everything from back home at first. As people moved to the new outreach, they took up more responsibility, remembering that the home committee was still there for reference if they wanted it. But the church back home always had its finger on the pulse of the fledgling church. The bishop made frequent calls and also arranged for ordained brethren from home to take their turns visiting.

Chapter 2

Naturally we think first of ordained leaders when we say "leaders." However, the ordained should in turn delegate responsibility. There should be an outreach committee, a building committee perhaps, and various leaders who take the burden off the minister. Not that ministers should divorce themselves from the decision-making process, but neither should they have to make all the decisions.

Remember in all of this that nothing oils the gears like love, and nothing strengthens the work like strength of character in the people involved. As William Penn once said, "Let men be good and the government can't be bad."

The stay-at-homes. There is something satisfying about being on the cutting edge of evangelism. But not everyone can be there. Some people must labor in the shadows, ready to say a word for the Lord but not having as many opportunities to do so as their friends "out there."

However, while outreach work *looks* more important than the work back home, it is clearly not so. Outreaches could hardly exist without the people back home.

For example, persons in outreach get telephone calls from Rod and Staff or other publishers, saying, "There's a family about thirty miles from you that called in to us yesterday. They have been getting our literature, and they wonder where they could find a congregation that thinks like us. We gave them your number. If they don't call you in a day or so, call them."

So the outreach begins, not with people in outreach, but with publishers. But who made it possible for publishers to publish? People like you and me who stayed home and wrote. People who went through everyday experiences and put them into print. They were not out on the battlefront. Perhaps we should say they were, but on a different battlefield.

Jesus recognized the value of quiet labor when He told His disciples, "Other men laboured, and ye are entered into their labours" (John 4:38). Although the twelve disciples had great

Catching the Vision

rewards for their work, the Lord had not forgotten His unnamed disciples. To them He would say, as He said to Nathanael, "When thou wast under the fig tree, I saw thee" (John 1:48).

Although you might not have the privilege to move to an outreach, you might get to visit there. Maybe you can help the work while you are there. For example, someone might be fixing up a house he just bought, and you can help either with the carpenter work and painting or with the cooking for the carpenter crew. For another example, you might be asked to visit school and lead in devotions or help tutor a child. If you visit over a weekend, maybe you can lead the singing or teach a Sunday school class.

It might dawn on you then that much of the work at an outreach is as humdrum as the work back home. Even at a mission that is on the leading edge of evangelism, someone has to stand on the back porch and shake out the dust mop.

There are other ways to help from behind the scenes. If workers at an outreach find some young boy or girl who needs a temporary home, maybe your family can take the child in. If the farmers at a new settlement experience tough times at first, maybe you can give an interest-free loan.

One more illustration. An insightful person wrote this tribute to women on the home front who dedicated time to sewing.

> I have learned to appreciate much more deeply the long labor and faithfulness of the thousands of women who have patiently toiled month after month in what often seems to be menial service. Certainly each of them could have found other, perhaps more pleasant, things to be occupied with all those days that they gave of themselves, generously and uncomplainingly. . . . I would be very glad to see and hear leaders of our church begin to help our "sewing" sisters to realize just how important what they are accomplishing really

is in the whole mission picture of our church. I think perhaps when their work is done, God will be able to say of them, "She hath done what she could." Will He be able to say that of all of us?[3]

The Decision to Go or Stay[4]

"Neither count I my life dear unto myself."
Acts 20:24

When the call comes for someone to go to an outreach, the person called might find himself in a dilemma. He might not seem to be getting any clear signals from God to help him know what to do. Besides, he might feel strong tugs within himself either to go or to stay, and he fears that what he *wants* to do clouds his understanding of what he *ought* to do. A young man facing one of those go-or-stay decisions confided to a friend, "I've often sung, 'I'll go where you want me to go, dear Lord; / I'll stay where you want me to stay.' Now I'm not sure if I knew what I was singing!"

One thing a person can do to make the decision easier is to cut away those reasons for going or staying that have no real connection to what God wants. First, let us consider what might be some not-so-good reasons people give when saying no to a call.

"I am so tied down." True, some people's duties tie them to the spot. They have good reason to say no when asked to move. We will look at that later. On the other hand, Elisha was tied down, farming, when Elijah called him. He left the farm. James and John were tied down with their fishing business when

---

[3] Wilma Yutzy, "Sewing Sisters Still Important," *Gospel Herald,* September 24, 1985, p. 671.

[4] Adapted from David L. Martin's, "The Decision to Go or Stay," *The Eastern Mennonite Testimony,* October 1989, pp. 5–7.

Catching the Vision

Jesus called them. They left their nets with their father. The fact is, people who are tied to responsibilities are the ones God calls. Those who have not committed themselves to anything do not have the qualities God wants.

"My friends think I should stay." Are the friends expressing what they seriously think is God's will, or are they simply expressing fondness for their friend? No one should let himself be kept at home because friends say, "We'll miss you." Anybody who is not missed at home will not be needed anywhere else. By the same token, no one should be put off because someone says, "The Lord has blessed your work right here. We'd be sorry to see you go." That is the kind of worker the people in outlying areas want. They do not want the kind the Lord has not blessed!

"My family needs me." Some families truly cannot spare anyone to go far away, because of their own pressing needs. For instance, invalid parents might keep their single children tied down through no fault or selfishness of their own. Nevertheless, there is another side to this. Certain children might need to realize what is hard for any child to realize—that their parents are too possessive of them. Mothers can put guilt on their children to the point that their children do not feel free to do God's will.

Young parents, let us take warning. The trouble with selfish parents starts when their children are young. Instead of thinking ahead to when their children are serving the Lord either near or far away, they are dreaming of reunions and grandchildren. Selfish dreams are hard to put away.

Brothers and sisters should also beware of expecting the single sister to do too much for the family. Yes, someone must take care of Mother. But must it be the unmarried daughter? Is it true that that is why God led her to stay unmarried—to take care of Mother? Maybe married children could take Mother in and do just as well as a single person, leaving their sister free to serve the Lord on the mission field.

Chapter 2

"I have moved often enough already." Humans have their limits. People who can never say no can end up running themselves ragged. But then again, we want to beware of telling the Lord what we will or will not do. Most of us have only first-graders' concepts of sacrifice compared to some heroes of God in the past (or present). Remember the saints of Hebrews 11 who "wandered about." Remember the apostle Paul who declared that he had "no certain dwellingplace." Remember also that Jesus said, "The Son of man hath not where to lay his head."

Actually, some sacrifices are only as painful as we make them. Some people enjoy moving from place to place. "Mind over matter," someone said. "If you don't mind, it doesn't matter."

Surely, there are many other reasons for staying instead of going, but this is a fair sampling.

Now let us look at some of these reasons again and think when they might actually be valid. Let us not be too casual about somebody else's sacrifice.

"I am tied down." Hardly anybody is so tied down that he cannot untie himself if he really must. But let us beware of thinking that some people are footloose and can easily drop things and run. Single people buy houses too, just as married people do. Sometimes they start new jobs and owe their employers a reasonable amount of time. Even those people who are willing to make a move are glad when others act as though they realize what all might be involved.

"My family needs me." We certainly believe it is right to break family ties to go to a mission field. We also believe something is wrong when a young woman cannot leave her mother. Many young single people understand this. Their real struggle comes, not when they are called to go, but when they are called to stay. It seems so unmissionary-minded to do chores back home on the farm. But to shoulder a load at home so that someone else in the family can serve the Lord in a special way—or simply to do much-needed chores at home, even though no one else in

Catching the Vision

the family is a missionary—can be the Lord's work too. Would you travel a thousand miles to take care of children, nurse an invalid, or help a needy family? Would you keep a missionary's records, mow his grass, fix his car, or cook his meals? Why not do these things at home if that is where God has called you?

"I have moved often enough already." Probably very few people who are called to move away bluntly say, "Sorry, I've moved often enough." That would not ring quite right! But can such a thing as moving too often actually be possible? Perhaps it can.

Single people, just because they are people, have homing instincts much as married people do. They appreciate married friends who think, "After all, if we as a family were to go, we would take each other. We would likely take the dishes and the children's toys and some furniture—maybe even Fido." It is far different for the single person who cannot take a family member or a piece of furniture with him. And since he must fit into some other family's patterns, he can't even take his own ways of doing things.

Does there not come a time in any person's life when he should be allowed to settle down? To move from place to place may be just fine for the single person when he is young. It might add spice to his life and teach him lessons on how to get along with people. But after ten or fifteen years, he may find it pleasant—even good for his emotional well-being—to be allowed to put down some roots.

Put yourself in the other person's place. One of the problems of living in many different places is that you do not completely belong to any one spot. You may not be a member of the congregation where you are living. When you return to your home church, the children have grown bigger, and you feel you have missed the most recent chapter at home—a chapter everyone knows but you. What is more, you will soon be off again, which means you do not dare settle down too much here.

Chapter 2

Of course it is hard to speak for everyone. No doubt, some people have made change a part of their life. But when others who have already tried to put down roots in several places become increasingly reluctant to pull up roots again, they should be understood.

"My friends think I should stay." Some of the best friends anyone has are the ordained men of his church. Usually when someone pours out his heart to them over a decision, they point out a few things to consider but then are careful to leave the final decision to the person involved. On those few occasions when they very strongly recommend one road or another, it is for good reasons. It would be foolish to disregard what they say. If you think that on this point, your minister's judgment is no better than yours is, beware. God has a way of respecting a church leader's word even if you do not. And He has a way of making that clear!

Other friends who are neither church leaders nor fathers and have no real authority might also have strong opinions on the subject. That is all right. Solomon said, "In the multitude of counsellors there is safety" (Proverbs 11:14). However, Solomon never meant that we must obey every one of our counselors. We would be running off in a dozen different directions. He did mean that a multitude of counselors helps us think of aspects and angles that we might not have thought of ourselves. "Have you considered waiting a year or two?" someone asks. Another says, "What about spending a week visiting the place you might work at, to get a better idea of what it is like before you make too many promises?" Finally, however, the decision falls on the would-be missionary himself.

Those who have had to make such decisions would suggest, "Pray about it. Do not just present the whole matter to God and then get up and walk away. Find a quiet spot and take time to think as well as to pray. Some things will occur to you that simply will not come to your mind as long as you are hurrying around. Maybe only one key thought will occur to you, but that will be all you need."

It does not all have to be decided in one session with God. If you save all your thinking for one special hour in which to make your decision, your mind might go blank when you get there. Let the decision grow on you over time.

These observations, finally, should help us think fairly from different angles about decisions we must make. It should also remind us that it is easier to be wise for other people than it is to be wise for ourselves. Let us not make decisions too quickly and easily for other people.

Chapter 3

First Decisions on the Field

Money

"For if there be first a willing mind, it is accepted according to that a man hath, and not according to that he hath not."

2 Corinthians 8:12

All questions about money boil down to just two: Where does the Lord want our money to come from? and Where does He want it to go?

Where it should come from. Let us not assume that the Lord will supply all our need with no planning, saving, or scraping on our part. Yes, the Bible teaches us to have faith in the almighty God. But faith and haphazardness are two different things. God places each of us here with limited resources in order to see what we do with them. We have to figure out our priorities. God's resources are unlimited, but He will not pour them on someone whose bookkeeping is careless.

It is important to work as a team. We are all in this together, including the people back home. We are told that George Mueller financed his orphanages, telling no one but God of his financial needs. Actually, friends prayed along with him, so there was more teamwork there than one might think at first. Many people contributed to the project with their money,

CHAPTER 3

some of them no doubt exercising faith that God in turn would supply their needs. So that speaks of teamwork too.

God wants to work with us now in the same way. In our churches, it takes everyone's faith and everyone's money to make an outreach work.

That is the way the people back home want it. When they say, "Make your needs known," they mean it. This does not mean you can sit around waiting for money to roll in from the home area. It does mean that if you do your part, others will too.

Feel free to suggest that you need things that are not money. Consider buying a shabby house (with the advice of people back home) with the understanding that they will try to send some young people to help fix it up.

Financial struggle is not all bad. The person who ventures into an outreach learns several things.

First, he does not have to maintain the living standard he was familiar with back home. In fact, perhaps he should try not to. The leaders at one church in an outlying area deliberately discourage their members from buying new pickups. They want to maintain a common, approachable image with which the average person can feel comfortable. The same principle applies to homes and furniture—a poor person should be able to walk in and not feel out of place. Once a person at an outreach has dropped some trappings of prosperity, he begins to wonder why people at home still have them.

Second, he is not too good to get help from his brethren, especially during the transition period, which might last a year or two—maybe even longer. He learns that it is more comfortable to give than to receive, and perhaps what he learns will make him more gracious in the future with people who must be on the receiving end.

Third, God will help him maintain a measure of independence, "for every man shall bear his own burden" (Galatians 6:5). People who get constant aid from the home church

First Decisions on the Field

do not always make out as well as people who must scratch. That is, people who are forced to supply at least some of their own needs learn good habits that serve them well both financially and spiritually. Charles Kingsley put it this way: "Thank God—every morning when you get up—that you have something to do which must be done, whether you like it or not. Being forced to work, and forced to do your best, will foster in you a hundred virtues which the idle never know."

Fourth, the outreach worker might realize for the first time what some people back home have been struggling with all along. Not just mission workers must live by faith. For many quiet saints, living by faith is business as usual.

A new worker should not render himself ineffective by getting into deep debt. The local deacon should make it his business to know if someone is hurting financially and should help with funds or with a loan or, perhaps best of all, with advice.

"Meeting the Financial Needs of Mission Workers"

God frequently calls workers into situations where it is difficult to meet one's financial and material needs. When this is the case, God intends that other Christians help supply these needs.

It is Scriptural for mission workers to have a trade. The apostle Paul exercised his tent-making skills from time to time, as a way to provide for his own needs (Acts 20:34). He considered this an asset, not a hindrance, to his spiritual ministry. Involvement in material responsibilities is beneficial to the physical and emotional well-being of mission workers. It likewise contributes to the effectiveness of their ministry, since most of the people they will witness to also need to work for a living. It is ideal when circumstances

Chapter 3

allow mission workers to earn at least a portion of their livelihood through material employment.

But what about the situations where this is not possible? How shall the financial needs be met when mission workers cannot secure an earning status, or when a missionary visa prohibits holding a job, or when it may take months or years for a worker to establish a project that will bring sufficient returns to support his family? If all of one's energies must be invested in making a living, mission interests usually suffer. Therefore, the sending body must be ready to assume responsibility for the financial needs of workers in the mission projects she takes up.

In practical terms, this means that some workers may need continued full support. Others may need full support at first and partial support as time passes and livelihood possibilities are discovered or developed. In some cases, workers may arrive at a self-support status. Obviously, these variations could create occasions for feelings of partiality. Christian maturity, confidence, charity, and forbearance are qualities that will help the work progress in spite of the variety of needs.

It is important for the administration to operate according to established policies and to maintain healthy communication with workers so that financial details do not become a liability to the cause of Christ. Financial support must be approached in a manner that is fair, retains human dignity and self-respect, and does not destroy personal initiative.

Further, the sending church must avoid the pitfall of providing unlimited support. Establishing a set amount of support is safer than promising to pay all worker expenses with no guidance given as to what is considered expense. However, workers deserve the security of the support of the sending body. "For the labourer is worthy of his hire" (Luke 10:7). Consideration also needs to be given to those who return from the field after a lifetime of service.

Mission workers can best meet the necessary changes and adjustments associated with a different culture and economic standard of living, when they are individuals who know how to live the simple, sacrificial lives of godly stewards, and are willing to do without many of the conveniences they may have been accustomed to having.[1]

Where it should go. As sure as you have an outreach, you will meet people who love to be reached out to, preferably with cash in hand. Sometimes helping people financially is appropriate; sometimes it is not.

Many financial questions arise about women who are one-parent heads of households. Each situation is different, but here are some more-or-less typical ones.

Situation: Amy A. has six young children and is in poor health. She has no sources of income. She is a church member.

Possible solution: After proper investigation, simply supply her needs.

"Simply?" someone says. "This solution raises more questions. What constitutes a need? And who decides what constitutes the need—Amy or the church?"

Maybe we should look at the husband–wife relationship for an answer. In a typical household, the husband provides the

---

[1] Paul Ebersole, "Meeting the Financial Needs of Mission Workers," *The Eastern Mennonite Testimony,* April 1990, pp. 4, 5.

Chapter 3

money and the wife goes shopping. They have to work out together how much she can afford to spend. The needs are obvious, but so are the limits. The limits seem to cramp them but teach them good lessons in values and priorities.

In Amy's case, the church could assume the role of a husband (preferably not the role of a father, unless Amy is obviously incompetent), explaining that unlimited aid will be good for no one. One could say, "After looking at the amount our own families live on, we think this figure is about right for you. It does not give you much margin for error, but if you are careful, it should work. Save your receipts, and if it turns out the figure is unrealistic, we can look at it again."

Are we expecting Amy to handle only the money needed for shopping while the church pays her bills for rent, electricity, water, sewer, and garbage? If we go back to the admittedly imperfect husband–wife analogy, we find that the arrangement varies. Sometimes the husband pays the bills; sometimes the wife does. In Amy's case, she is, after all, the head of her household, and it seems right to give her a stipulated amount out of which she pays her own bills. She might be more careful to turn off the lights if she knows the saving will be hers. (Are we not all like that?)

On the other hand, suppose Amy already has twelve pairs of shoes for herself but no milk or eggs, and that pattern is likely to continue. Then the church has little choice but to take charge of her finances as much as necessary, while doing it as respectfully as possible.

Situation: Bonnie B. has a source of income but has given up trying to make sense of her finances. She has changed her telephone number to elude bill collectors and has begun throwing statements away unopened.

Possible solution: Help her make a budget—perhaps a highly tentative one at first until she learns to save her receipts and see where her money goes. If she has enough income to reach, point

First Decisions on the Field

this out to her. By making frank arrangements with her creditors to pay off her debts over a period of time, she might have the satisfaction of working them all off without outside help.

The church might need to say a word on Bonnie's behalf to the creditors. Usually creditors react reasonably when they discover that church people are working with the problem.

Situation: Cindy C. must dedicate most of her time to her children, but her health is good, and she has a little time at odd moments to work. She has no outside source of income.

Possible solution: Investigate the options. Would Cindy feel comfortable doing some ironing for people? Could she take the children with her to help clean church? Can she do any lawn or garden care? Does she have a skill such as bookkeeping that some businessman could benefit from? Odd earnings will not take care of all her needs, but it will give her a sense of satisfaction to be doing at least something toward earning her keep. This is true even if church people give her a very high wage for doing her work—a hundred dollars for a thirty-five-dollar job might not be out of line.

Any job, of course, should not be of the make-work type and so simple that it is insulting.

Situation: Donna D. attends church frequently and professes to be a Christian. She asks for prayer because she has expensive doctor bills and car repairs. She never asks for money—exactly—but neither does she ask questions about what the church believes.

Possible solution: It cannot be a mistake to pray for Donna; that is what she asked for. Do her favors as the Lord leads, but make no commitments.

Situation: Elaine E.'s husband has moved across town and supports his wife less and less. Elaine is a church member.

Possible solution: Make haste slowly. Elaine's husband should sense his responsibility. But how will he if someone takes that responsibility off his shoulders too soon? The church told one

Chapter 3

such Elaine, "We'll let you go to the limit, but we won't let you starve." She understood.

Elaine should not remain forever in a state of near-destitution, but the Lord has ways of working these things out.

Other situations arise as well. Frank is a ne'er-do-well, and his children are following his example. There is a one-eyed teddy bear in their forsythia bush and an old sink under it and . . . Frank cannot keep a steady job, and he has run short of money. He has asked the deacon for help.

One solution may be to tie money to improvements in Frank's own sense of responsibility. Maybe you could propose the same thing Abraham Lincoln proposed to his stepbrother: "For every dollar that you will, between this and the first of May, get for your own labor . . . I will then give you one other dollar."

These days when couples are separating because they find themselves in adulterous relationships, churches may need to help cushion financial blows that come with separation. Some couples will be able to handle their own money affairs, but others will need more from the church than just direction.

A question arises when someone who is interested in the church has been on welfare. Shall we encourage him or her to stop getting welfare payments? After all, we believe the church should support her own! True, but is the person in question really the church's own? A go-slow approach is probably best. Not that we begrudge giving our help to people, even non-church members. It is just that we cannot be responsible for every need that might be out there, and trying to do so might be bad for both them and us.

Yes, you can help people too much. Years ago in a West Virginia community, people walked to church. They put forth effort and initiative to get there. Then someone moved into the community with a van and began hauling people to church. Result: fewer people came. It had been made too easy. Evidently, people had lost their independence and sense of self-respect.

First Decisions on the Field

As we draw people into the church, we want them to develop the same mentality that we ourselves supposedly already have—the concept that the church is not a welfare institution. Simply handing bills over to the church is a foreign concept to us because the responsibility falls on the individual and his God, and the church is merely one of God's instruments to supply the individual's needs. "Honour widows that are widows indeed. But if any widow have children or nephews, let them learn first to shew piety at home, and to requite their parents: for that is good and acceptable before God" (1 Timothy 5:3, 4).

At the same time the Bible speaks of "the daily ministration" and points out the trouble a church can run into if this is neglected (Acts 6:1). It also says, "But whoso hath this world's good, and seeth his brother have need, and shutteth up his bowels of compassion from him, how dwelleth the love of God in him? My little children, let us not love in word, neither in tongue; but in deed and in truth" (1 John 3:17, 18).

Finally, "Pure religion and undefiled before God and the Father is this, To visit the fatherless and widows in their affliction, and to keep himself unspotted from the world" (James 1:27).

Housing

"Your heavenly Father knoweth that ye have need of all these things."

Matthew 6:32

Be prepared for some frustrations before everyone is settled. One brother, working hard to locate suitable properties, ran into so many roadblocks that he finally said, "How many doors must close before we take the hint?" But the search continued! Eventually everyone found a home.

In the search for housing, it is important not to panic. If some other buyer slips in ahead of you on a property you like, this is not the end of the end. The other party might not be

Chapter 3

able to "swing it," or he might simply change his mind. At one point, someone called this writer and said, "The blue house is gone." It was not. Church people bought it, and the outreach has been using it ever since.

If the other party does buy a property you want, all is still not lost. The Lord is directing it all. He closes doors; He opens doors. As any realtor can assure you, other properties will come on the market. One of them might be as good as or better than the one that passed you by. It happens all the time.

Neither is all lost if you find yourself committed to a property and learn that it will not do. Go back to the people involved and ask for an honorable release or ask what your responsibility is in such a case.

In the community where your outreach is located, the housing picture might be quite different from what it is back home. You might expect to rent a decent place on terms like ones you have been familiar with, only to find that rental rates are out of sight. And money is not the only hurdle. One brother thought he had finally located a place to rent, until the rental agency told him his family was too big for the house. That was that.

Maybe in some localities, renting makes more sense than buying, especially while you are still feeling your way and have not yet determined where your church and school will be. However, many times buying is the way to go if you have the resources to do so.

Try to get a house that has more space than you absolutely need at the moment. A spare room is convenient so that if company comes every weekend, you do not always need to shift your children around.

But by this we are simply holding up the ideal. Not everyone will be able to afford or locate the ideal. Besides, learning to take turns and make do can have advantages too.

When locating a house, remember the children. One couple living in New York City never bought a bicycle for their son because they knew someone on the street would simply take it from him. That in itself would have been sad, but children living in godless environments can lose more than bicycles. They can lose their virtue. In the process they can help to undermine the mission effort instead of helping to support it. If the Lord leads you to a house that you do not quite like but that sits off to the side a bit, it may be your children He has in mind.

Regarding the actual moving, here is just one suggestion: a committee responsible to help you move can be a great help. Committee members feel more comfortable asking someone to donate his truck to help you move than you would.

A Sanctuary

"And on the sabbath we went out of the city by a river side, where prayer was wont to be made."
Acts 16:13

Sailboats and haystacks have made good pulpits; mountainsides and riversides have made good churches. They remind us that "God is a Spirit" and that the most important thing about worshiping Him is not the sanctuary but, rather, worshiping "in spirit and in truth." But the sky is not always blue, and as a rule you will be worshiping under a roof.

The first while. Should you rent or build? You might want to rent or lease a building until you get a feel for the area and know for a fact where you want to build. A proper church building might have to wait for a while. But outreach workers worshiping in temporary locations have shown great ingenuity in making do with what they had.

One outreach worshiped in a Grange hall for a while. At least it put a roof over their heads. Such an arrangement would mean paying for the privilege and setting up and taking away folding chairs. Another small difficulty with renting a public building could be that community people get the

Chapter 3

impression that the work is temporary.

Another outreach located a day-care facility they could use for weekend services. In lieu of paying rent, they made repairs and improvements to the building.

An outreach in northwest Pennsylvania met for two months in a kitchen cabinet show room.

Another new congregation found an old school that worked for their school and also doubled for their Sunday services.

At another outreach, the people found an added-to mobile home. Accommodations were so tiny that one of the rooms served as living room, bedroom, church, and school.

One church started out by leasing an old dance hall.

> The building was old, drafty, and hard to heat. The benches were improvised from planks and boxes and not very comfortable. They were also not very stable, as several of the early teacher workers have informed us; sometimes an unruly student managed to upset the bench he was using and even succeeded in causing a whole row of benches to fall down. But these things did not hinder the attendance nor dampen the enthusiasm of the workers.[2]

Once in a while the church building sits waiting for you. At one new outreach, the people found an unused Lutheran church they leased for about eight years before building their own church. Another outreach bought an old church building when the former church group moved to another location. Still another new congregation found a church building that had been built two years before but had never had a permanent congregation.

The Orwin, Pennsylvania, outreach had an interesting

---

[2] Norman F. Wine, *The History of Miners Village Mennonite Church* (Lebanon, PA: Norman F. Wine, c. 1995), p. 25.

First Decisions on the Field

experience. The brethren located an old church whose owners offered it to them rent-free. They were told they could just use it. But the brethren knew they would be doing renovations on the building and did not want any legal entanglements. Therefore, they went through the necessary procedures to buy it. They put an ad in the paper about their intentions. They made contact with all the heirs and had them sign off. The heirs had one stipulation—that the Mennonites would not sell the building for anything but a church before the year 2000. Finally, the church bought the place for a dollar. Everyone was happy.

But later they built a new church at a better location and wanted to sell this one. Although the year 2000 had come, some older relatives of the heirs felt bad. The feeling was, "The community gave you this building for a church, and now you want to sell it!"

In the end, good feeling prevailed. The church people offered the building back to the community for approximately the amount they had put into renovations. They also offered to sell it to one of the heirs. Neither of those deals went through (someone else bought it), but at least the church had made their generous intentions clear.

In another case, the outreach met in a large garage they divided into two rooms, one for a school and one for an all-purpose room that included services. They installed restrooms, put up wall paneling they had bought from a mobile home dealer, did some painting, and had carpet installed. The effect was cozy. Ventilation was no problem in summer; they could simply raise the big garage doors to whatever level they pleased.

Meeting in a home or garage at first can actually be an advantage. Some community people will feel more free to visit there than in a church building. Even after erecting a regular church, it might be a good idea to continue to have home Bible studies. At one outreach, the workers held Bible studies in

Chapter 3

people's homes until the meetings became crowded. So they decided to have the Bible studies in church. At this they lost people who had been coming to the home Bible studies. If the group gets too big, dividing and having two Bible studies might be a good answer.

First services. Is space at a premium? There are folding podiums that look a bit like wooden brief cases when collapsed. They come in handy when church is in someone's living room.

It is understood that you will not have all levels of Sunday school classes at first. In fact, you might have only an adult class with everyone sitting in, including children. Later you might divide into two or three classes as you have more students and more teachers.

Those weekends when the only preacher is gone can be rather awkward. One thing to do is have Sunday school as usual and fill in the time with some extra singing. This should seldom happen.

If people are coming from quite a distance at first, you will want to have lunch for them after church—maybe supper too. After a time when the congregation moves closer to each other, you will probably phase out the fellowship lunches, having them only for special occasions. Visitors from the community get to see the congregation in a different light when they are invited into individual homes.

Buying a lot. The varying gifts of the church become evident when a group goes out to buy a lot. A brother who preaches good sermons might nevertheless have very little helpful advice about buying a property. Other brethren can shine here.

Some considerations follow:

1. Will you want the church along a highway? You want some publicity, and you get it free that way.

2. Do you want a property on a hillside so that you can have ground-level access to school in the basement?

3. Are most members living close to your proposed site? If

First Decisions on the Field

church is too far away, members may have difficulty persuading their friends and neighbors to come to church.

4. How is the well? Or what prospects are there for drilling a good one? The need for a good drain field has to be considered too. Remember, much water flows on all-day-meeting Sundays.

5. Have enough space on your lot. One church was boxed in between the highway and the property of a neighbor who did not want to sell. Suddenly the property did sell—but not to the church. The new neighbor was good-natured enough. He would have been glad to sell part of his land to the church. Then he discovered that if he subdivided his land, he would have to donate the frontage of his property to the highway. This he did not want to do. The moral for new churches: buy right the first time.

6. Do local ordinances make building on the proposed lot unfeasible? Suppose you find an ideal spot for a church along some quiet country road. Will the increased traffic mean that you have to pay for upgrading the road all the way in from the main highway? That could be so expensive as to be prohibitive.

7. Are you close enough to town to get town water? Occasionally this question is important.

8. After you have bought a property, time might pass before you can build on it. Figure a year and a half of paperwork before you begin to build. In the meantime, keep up the property; do not let it look as if no one cares.

Building the building. Ask friends back home what they would do differently if they were building their church over again. Consult the sisters too. You might get some interesting answers.

The trend today is away from long and narrow auditoriums. A more nearly square floor plan gives the building a broader entrance at the rear. The vestibule should be large enough to reduce congestion as people are putting on their coats and heading out the door, talking as they go.

Chapter 3

For some reason people like to stand in small corners. Do not build a bottleneck between the mother's room door and the restroom door where the girls will congregate. Consider building the mother's room next to the restroom with a door leading directly from room to room. Make the mother's room big enough for an expanding congregation.

Have a varicolored carpet to avoid showing dirt. A light, solid color will be unpopular long before the carpet wears out.

Consider stretching your budget to build the whole building at once, rather than doing it by stages. Some brethren will tell you it is best to move ahead while people still have high interest in the new work. Now is the time to take offerings and to appeal for people's labor. A few years down the road, other works will be starting, and the edge of excitement about your work will not quite be there.

On the other hand, if the interest and funds are local, you might want to build in stages. Have a dual-purpose building at first. On Sundays, move the school desks to one side and set up folding chairs. Later build an addition and have separate facilities.

Consider the way people build in this new locality. If they do not build basements, why not? They might have good reasons. Beware of coming in with new ideas from home, expecting to show your new neighbors (who have lived in the area for years) a thing or two. One brother from the East built a basement in the Southwest, but when rain came, the ground heaved up under his basement floor with such force that it broke the center support of the house. At least it was not his church.

However you build it, take the congregation along each step of the way. A committee is fine, but the committee should present the various steps to the people. When deciding the main color of the auditorium, for example, the committee can narrow the choices down to perhaps three colors and then have the congregation decide.

First Decisions on the Field

Jobs and Businesses

"Whatsoever thy hand findeth to do, do it with thy might."
Ecclesiastes 9:10

You might want to work as an employee for a while. Setting up your own business first thing might succeed—or it might not. The old assumptions that held true back home might not work in another state or country. You might not know the market; how do you know people will want to buy your picnic tables or your tomatoes for the price you are used to getting? You might not altogether understand the climate; how do you know that the kind of sweet corn that you used in your truck patch back home will thrive in your new location?

On the other hand, whether knowledgeable or not, a person might need to start up a business rather than seek employment. The brethren at Alturas, California, found it just the opposite of what is suggested here. They were virtually forced to set themselves up in business because there were hardly any jobs.

As time goes on and you set up a business, you might want to provide employment for community people. It can touch their lives as nothing else does. One young community man, challenged by his Christian employer on what the Bible teaches, commented, "If it weren't for you, I wouldn't care what the Bible teaches."

School

"In heaven their angels do always behold the face of my Father."
Matthew 18:10

Planning curriculum for the first year of school could be awkward. Children might be moving in from three or four different localities. Even if they all were using the same curriculum

CHAPTER 3

publisher at their former schools, they might be out of step with each other. Maybe at first a few of them will have to take a course over again that they took last year in their previous school.

Teachers should be flexible and good-natured. They might find themselves crammed into a small trailer and have to shift their chair every time someone opens the door. They might suddenly have to accommodate extra students partway through the year.

One school taxed the ingenuity of its teachers pretty heavily. Children who did not know English kept moving in. Since they were at different levels of knowledge, the teachers had to individualize a good bit at first. Later they tried to slip the students into a grade level suited to them. Incidentally, the teachers' main method of teaching English was to teach the children to read.

The teachers solved the problem of numbers as follows:

> Classroom space and textbooks are rather scarce because of the explosive growth of the school. We are running the school in shifts. Four classes are in session in the morning from 8:00 A.M. to 1:00 P.M. The three afternoon classes meet from 1:30 P.M. to 6:30 P.M. It does make for an efficient use of classrooms and textbooks—maybe too efficient."[3]

By the way, the odds are against you if you try to set up a school in some distant locality without appointing some strong personalities to be on the spot. Avoid long-distance administrating if at all possible. Wait until you have moved in with your church and can administer it with local people. Absentee school boards can be impotent.

Another warning. If someone asks you to teach school at

---

[3] The Robert Eby family, "Northwest News: Letter From the Field," *The Eastern Mennonite Testimony,* May 1997, p. 9.

First Decisions on the Field

some lonely outreach where there is not a local church, say no. One outreach tried to set up a school like this and asked a teacher from a distance to serve there. When that teacher's church leaders discovered the scheme, they declared they would diametrically oppose the arrangement until the school planners came up with a better plan! Thank God for such brethren.

The distant but interested. What can you do for interested people who live an hour or more away from the church and school? Usually they can manage to visit church on weekends. This arrangement might do for a while if their children are preschoolers. But school is another story, with no easy answers.

Shall they homeschool, whether the parents are qualified or not? Shall they come to school once a week and homeschool the rest of the time? Shall the children board several days a week near the school? Shall they commute to school every day despite the time and expense involved? If they do, shall some young person do the afternoon run?

In one case, a family had involvements that kept them from moving closer to the church for at least a year. Therefore, the church proposed that the family spend extended weekends in the locality of the church. On Mondays the children could get some instruction and assignments for the following week. When they could not come to the church, someone would go to their home on weekends to give the needed direction. Through the week they kept in touch by fax machine. "A poor setup is better than none," and this at least was a setup.

In another case, the church leaders studied a brother's situation and finally decided they would not be starting a church or school in his area. They recommended that he move closer to the existing church and school. His plight drew their sympathy because they knew the move would involve financial loss. However, he made that move.

Incidentally, asking people to move from one community to another can turn out to be an advantage for them. They

CHAPTER 3

might get away from familiar influences that retard their spiritual progress. One man moved to a distant community to join the Mennonites, later moving back when the Mennonites started a congregation in his original area. He says he doubts he would have made the break from his old life if he had not moved out for a while.

Coaching a non-Mennonite school. When a large group of Pentecostals from Russia moved into Canada, it soon became evident they were not prepared to teach their own children and would be sending their children to public school. One of the brethren saw this and quickly stepped in. He guided the Russians in setting up their own schools and served as one of their teachers, also helping to bring in other Mennonite teachers. (A Mennonite congregation was close enough for the teachers to attend.) As time moved on, the Russians became more knowledgeable and confident and began to supply their own teachers.

There are hazards to this approach. Teachers who immerse themselves too much in day-to-day life with people can find themselves identifying too much with them. This can lead them to become dissatisfied with their original church.

However, let us not perceive problems that do not exist. Sometimes we might be tempted to ask, "If we can't make Mennonites out of those people, what are we doing there in the first place?" We need to remember that if we help to raise or preserve the spiritual level of people, whoever they may be, we are doing a good work even if we do not have more Mennonites to show for it. It is sometimes enough if we are "the salt of the earth."

A Mennonite school with a difference. Besides coaching a non-Mennonite school, Mennonites can set up and run their own school expressly for a foreign group. In this case they would keep a somewhat tighter rein on the school.

Families who want to send their children must be sifted.

First Decisions on the Field

The fact that they are enthusiastic today could mean little or nothing six months down the road. Those last three months to finish out the term can be a long, long time if a few parents have become disgruntled and a few students have become insufferable.

A constitution for such a school would look like the following. Notice that the dress standards are somewhat less definitive than those of a full-fledged Mennonite school, but they are certainly considerably higher than those of a public school.

CONSTITUTION AND BYLAWS OF THE NEWTOWN CHRISTIAN DAY SCHOOL

ARTICLE I STATUS

The school is a nonprofit organization supported by freewill contributions of interested persons. We shall not accept financial assistance from the state. The school is a church-operated organization established for the following purpose:

ARTICLE II PURPOSE

1. To practice the Bible principle that the child shall be taught in a godly environment with a Bible-centered curriculum.

2. To develop and bring into expression the child's God-given talents for use in spiritual and secular activities.

3. To assist the students in acquiring skills in Christian thinking and communication.

4. To teach useful subjects, conveying correct Bible emphasis, which will equip the students to fulfill their responsibilities in life, thus making a contribution to the church and society.

5. To teach that the Bible is the only Word of

Chapter 3

God, that it is inspired by the Holy Spirit, and that it is practical and important and speaks to all areas of life.

6. To teach a respect for authority, both religious and secular.

ARTICLE III FINANCES

The cost of operating the school includes the cost of curriculum, the teachers' wages, the cost of owning or renting a building, and the upkeep of the building. This is the responsibility of the parents.

ARTICLE IV STUDENTS

Students attending shall submit themselves to the order of the school as outlined in the following school standards, as well as to any other restrictions the teacher and board see necessary to enforce. Parents are to help the students to willingly observe all rules (or standards) of the school. Children who are disrespectful, rebellious, or uncooperative shall be subject to forfeiture of school privileges.

ARTICLE V ATTENDANCE

Parents must take the responsibility to see that the children are in school. If more than three days total are missed in one school year, the child will be subject to possible suspension. Sick days will not be subject to this rule, and possible exceptions could be made if properly cleared by the board and teachers. Pupils shall submit excuse cards signed by the parents for all absences from school, including tardiness and early afternoon absences. Habitual tardiness will not be allowed.

First Decisions on the Field

SCHOOL STANDARDS

1. School shall open with a devotional period each morning.

2. Television and radio will not be permitted in the homes of students attending this school.

3. The school shall have authority over all pupils from the time of their arrival at school, including playground activities, until their departure after dismissal.

4. Pupils shall not leave the school grounds at any time without the teacher's permission.

5. Parents shall be responsible for any careless or deliberate breaking or destroying of books, desks, windows, or other school property.

6. Books and games are not to be brought to school without being cleared with the teachers or school board.

DRESS STANDARDS

Parents shall provide simple, modest clothing and shoes. Loud styles and colors shall not be tolerated. Jewelry, gold, and silver shall not be worn.

FOR BOYS: Pullover T-shirts and shirts with writing or pictures will not be allowed. Hair shall be properly cut and combed.

FOR GIRLS: Dresses shall be long and full enough to come well below the knees at all times. Low-necked dresses shall not be worn. Girls shall wear their hair uncut and neatly combed in pony tails or braids, or put up into a bun when the veiling is worn. Bows shall not be worn.

This constitution reflects the concept that there is a limit to how fast we can take people. In one school for newcomers from a communist country, the Mennonite administrators

CHAPTER 3

insisted on such quick and rigid conformity to dress codes that one patron remarked, "It's just like communism!" Accusations like that may or may not be factual, but certainly we want to keep it from being true.

Regular Mennonite schools. Most schools we operate are full-fledged denominational schools for our own children, and we expect the people who patronize them to be church supporters if not members. Consideration for nonmember families attending our schools should be given only for those who are showing an interest in the church. Before we accept children from nonmember families, we will want to sit down and discuss a few items with the parents.

Ask them, for example, why they want to come to our school. If all they want is to escape some problem in the last school they attended, they are probably not suitable candidates.

Ask them what their concept of school government is. What about corporal punishment, for example? Discuss with them any problem they might have with school standards.

Are they willing to do away with television and radio, to eliminate that influence from the school?

In all this, remember that school is not primarily a mission field, even though it can work as such sometimes. If we admit into our schools children who bring wrong influences, we might end up losing our own children.

Homeschooling. Eventually the homeschooling issue will arise. If people ask you what you think of it, the following observations may be helpful.

> There are also some disadvantages to home schooling. Not all parents have the expertise to teach all the necessary school subjects, and some parents tend to major on the subjects they personally enjoy, at the expense of teaching other vital subjects. Also, not everyone has the ability to communicate academics in an understandable way. . . .

First Decisions on the Field

> What are the advantages of traditional classroom instruction? The teacher is able to give his whole attention and energy to his teaching task, uninterrupted by domestic duties. The children can also benefit from the group structure. They can learn the value of an orderly, disciplined schedule and atmosphere. The traditional approach also helps to produce children with a well-rounded education.[4]

Most conservative Mennonite churches have no homeschoolers as members. This is not because they view homeschooling as wrong in every situation but because they have something rather unique as a church that they would like to preserve—an emphasis on teamwork. With everyone patronizing church schools, it is easier to "be of the same mind in the Lord" (Philippians 4:2).

Local Laws
"Obey magistrates."
Titus 3:1

Local regulations can conceal snags especially frustrating to someone who has moved in from another state or country. He makes matters worse if he naively assumes that regulations will be the same in the new locality as in the old. "You need a permit to cut down a tree in rural Guatemala or to haul lumber or a cow in a trailer. But generally no permit is needed to build a house."[5] Even in the States or Canada, there might be regulations one never thought of.

---

[4] Michael S. Martin, "Relating to the Home School Movement; Part 1," *The Christian Contender,* January 1993, p. 10.

[5] Harry M. Erb, "Guatemala Facts," *The Eastern Mennonite Testimony,* May 1987, p. 9.

Chapter 3

What about water, for example? One outreach bought a property only to discover that since they would be having more than twenty-five people more than sixty days out of a year, they would fall into a new category. They would have to conform to almost as many water regulations as if they were supplying a whole town. This involved periodic water inspections (monthly, yearly, tri-yearly) that would cost over a thousand dollars a year, and this without any guarantee that the costs would not go up. In this case, the church worked with the local water association in an effort to reduce costs somewhat.

What should be our attitude toward regulations?

In preparation for this book, contributors were asked, "Did you have trouble with local laws and regulations?" This writer sympathizes with the brother who replied, "No, we just obeyed them. Too many people feel that they can ignore laws that do not seem reasonable to them. This will destroy the testimony of an outreach very quickly."

There is another side to this though. Sometimes it is practically impossible to be legal. For example, the law in your state might say that if you have more than twelve students in your school, your building must meet certain fire safety regulations and have so many exits, a ceiling just so high, a stipulated number of windows and fluorescent lights, and so on. If you are temporarily holding school in a rented building, you cannot do all of this.

No one understands better than agents of the law that the law must be flexible. A police officer once illustrated it by drawing a simple line on a piece of paper. "Here's the law," he said. "Sometimes we bend a little your way, and sometimes you bend a little our way." Jesus pointed out that even the law of God has a reasonable amount of "give" in it (Matthew 12:1–5).

One group of brethren working to buy a property hinted to officials that their school would be in violation of local codes for a time. "You won't come looking for us, will you?" one brother

First Decisions on the Field

asked. They did not. However, the officials kept the right to pursue the matter if the school became a public nuisance.

"Get it as legal as you can as soon as you can" seems like a good motto to go by. Just remember that our sons and daughters are growing up fast and watching everything we do. Younger generations have a tendency to snatch up the irregularities of their fathers and run with them, and we do not want to instill in them disrespect for the law.

Incidentally, we do not realize what officials have to go through with some of the other people they meet. After one Mennonite outreach presented their plans at a presubmission conference, one of the officials called them the politest group they had ever met. It was an indication that many others come with a chip on their shoulder and are difficult to deal with.

In some ways, rules are a nuisance; we all know that. So is the man down the street who cannot be pled with and will not change his ways until there *are* some rules.

An illustration of adjusting our plans to obey the laws of the land took place in the Bahamas:

> On Monday at noontime an immigration officer accompanied by a police officer appeared at the guest house where the brethren were lodging and informed them that they are working illegally and must stop immediately or else face imprisonment and deportation. The charge was that the brethren were involved in "gainful employment" (unlawful for foreigners without a special permit). The fact that their labor was all donated and that they were working on our own mission house seemed to make no difference. . . .
>
> After interviews with Andros Island officials on Tuesday and finally with officials in Nassau on Wednesday . . . , it was decided that our brethren would need to refrain from manual labor. They

CHAPTER 3

could, however, supervise the local help which was being employed. Our brethren then immediately engaged additional help, and by the time of their departure . . . , the house was nearly ready to be occupied.

Also discussed during the Wednesday interview was the establishing of a church. Our brethren were left with the impression that our church would need to be registered in the Bahamas and also associated with the Bahama Council of Churches to be privileged to baptize and receive members. Counsel with a local lawyer, however, indicated that their Constitution would not necessarily make such demands. He did advise though that we obtain some type of recognition and that for the present we have services on an informal basis.[6]

Loopholes are not altogether out of place:

One church would have had to hire a professional electrician to wire a house on the church property—if the church had owned the house. For some reason, it had been registered as sold to the pastor. During the interim before that was corrected, the pastor could legally be his own electrician. This brother knew little about wiring a house, but according to the law, as long as he helped at least nominally, his friends who knew more than he did could do most of the work.

Sometimes there seems to be no satisfactory solution:

Trying to get exemption from insurance, Mennonites in a southwestern state appealed to the government but were turned down because there were not enough families in their churches. So they took out insurance with the idea that they

---

[6] Lester H. Weaver, "Bahamas News: Called Into Question," *The Eastern Mennonite Testimony,* August 1983, p. 120.

would not collect if they had an accident. However, when accidents happened, it did not work out that way. The Mennonite would say, "Yes, I'm insured, but I prefer to pay the damage myself." The other person would say, "Can you pay?" The Mennonite: "Well, if I can't, my church will help me out." The other person: "I don't want to deal with you or with your church. Show me your insurance card." This not only kept the system from working, but it also tempted the Mennonites to depend on their insurance instead of on God and His people.

Some people have found a way to pay back to the insurance company what it pays on their behalf. This not only frees their consciences but also keeps their insurance rates to a minimum because any accidents they have do not go on their record.

Sometimes the stand that Christians take leads to an impasse, at least temporarily:

> The possibility of some sort of alternative service for our young brethren came to a screeching halt when the president of Paraguay refused to sign the necessary papers.[7]

Sometimes we must discipline a member if he cooperates with the government:

> A former church member is now mayor of El Edén and is the one responsible to order the community members to participate in the civil defense. . . . Having been excommunicated from the church because he took the office of mayor after having promised not to, he is now bitter

---

[7] The Lawrence Martin family, "Paraguay News: Letter From the Field," *The Eastern Mennonite Testimony,* July 1996, p. 8.

[8] Lester H. Weaver, "Guatemala News," *The Eastern Mennonite Testimony,* August 1983, p. 121.

CHAPTER 3

toward the church.[8]

Finding our way through some of these issues takes patient negotiation:

In British Columbia about 1990, a law passed requiring all private schools to register with the province if they wanted to continue as a school. This brought visions of Russian registered churches to mind—not an unworthy concern, since our schools are considered to be a church function.

Our leaders held off and voiced their concerns to the proper officials. At one point they traveled to Victoria, the British Columbia capital, and explained what they stood for. "If worse came to worst," they said, "we will have to leave the province." (An official told them afterwards, "That shook all Victoria!") The government then made some adjustments. The director of independent schools explained to our people that they could choose to come under a nonfunded classification so that the government would not have jurisdiction over curriculum, teachers, or students.

One of the church leaders reported afterwards, "We informed the representative from the Ministry of Education that if these explanations were documented from their department, we would give serious consideration to cooperating with them. We have now received a letter documenting these items and believe it is proper for us to proceed in requesting classification for the schools here."[9]

One way to proceed—perhaps a questionable one—is simply to move ahead without asking questions:

In one state that required insurance, the brethren simply used the cards issued by their church and said as little about it as possible. Other brethren questioned that "system," but at

---

[9] David G. Burkholder, "British Columbia School Registration Report," *The Eastern Mennonite Testimony,* August 1991, p. 9. (See *EMT* Sept. 1989, p. 9, for background.)

First Decisions on the Field

the time of this writing, they had not run into trouble.

In another state, the church started a school without asking questions. Eventually the truant officer stopped in but saw that the children were busy at their desks. They got away with it. But in retrospect one of the brethren admits that, in his judgment, what they did was really not quite proper.

Another outreach did the opposite. They met with the local school director, told him who they were, and had a friendly visit. The local school office wanted statistical information about the families attending the Mennonite school, and this the school patrons supplied. Relationships have been cordial ever since.

In all these matters, we must operate not only from the head but also from the heart. The Lord will not bless us if we blunder along without planning, thinking, and praying.

Chapter 4

Reaching the Community

God's people in Bible times found various ways to reach the community. Jonah simply shouted his message on the street (Jonah 3:4). John the Baptist did the opposite. Rather than entering cities, he preached in the wilderness, and people streamed out to him (Mark 1:4, 5). Both ways worked well.

But not every way of trying to reach the community works well. Lot tried to reach his community by sitting in the city gates; he lost some of his family in the overthrow of Sodom and barely escaped himself (Genesis 19). In this chapter, we will look at methods generally thought to be safe and effective. Yet here and there we will touch the question, How can we reach the community in such a way that it actually touches people's lives and enriches our own, rather than destroying us?

Efforts by the Church

"Then pleased it the apostles and elders, with the whole church, to send chosen men of their own company."

Acts 15:22

Public meetings. One way to measure community interest is to hold meetings in a tent or public hall. Naturally, such meetings do more than serve as a thermometer of public interest. They are a way of spreading the Gospel, even if only a

CHAPTER 4

handful of community people attend.

Besides praying for the Lord's direction on the work, what can you do to let people know you are in the community? Several ways are bulk mailings of programs, distribution of invitations, ads in the paper, and postings on public bulletin boards.

Bulk mailings. You can buy a bulk-mailing permit at the local post office. Though a bit expensive, it gives you the right to print a special note on the corner of the back of your program something like the following:

> US Postage
> **PAID**
> Standard A Mail
> Permit #23
> Berrytown, WA

The post office employees can help you get the format right.

With a bulk-mailing permit, you can bring several hundred programs to the post office and mail them at a reduced rate to any or all of the local routes and boxholders. The permit will probably last a year, meaning you can do a bulk mailing more than once per permit. You will want to mail quite a few; otherwise, your savings on postage will be eaten up by what you paid to get a permit in the first place. Do your arithmetic.

If all of this is too troublesome, you can find in the yellow pages a mailing service that already has a bulk-mailing permit and will be happy to mail out your programs. A mailing service prints address labels as well as doing the folding, inserting, collating, and so on. The cost varies, depending on how much you ask the service to do. If there is much hand labor involved, naturally the charge will be higher. Maybe you want to do a partial mail preparation and let the service do the rest. For cost effectiveness, bring in several thousand pieces.

By the way, maybe you can reduce mailing costs even further by applying for status as a nonprofit organization. Ask your post office for a form to see if you qualify. Your nonprofit

Reaching the Community

status should last indefinitely without a yearly renewal.

Christian publishing companies sometimes agree to assist congregations in making contact with people in their area.

Naturally, you will have your own personal list of interested people to whom you will mail individual programs.

Ads in the paper. If you are uncertain of yourself here, you can fax or mail to the advertising department of the newspaper a tentative ad along with your telephone number. Ask the ad department to get back to you so you can work out the details together. They will probably advise you not to run your ad in the classifieds but rather to put it with the other church news. They will recommend that you run the ad more than one day.

Results of advertising. Despite all your efforts, you may expect only a small fraction of the people who saw your invitation actually to respond. This might not mean that you should advertise less but, rather, more, to make that small fraction more worthwhile.

Think of it this way. You are already spending a considerable amount for the meeting—several hundred dollars for the meeting hall, another few hundred for reimbursing speakers. You have people investing considerable time to come from a distance and take part. Why then shall you cut corners on letting people know you are there?

Of course, if the response is minimal even after advertising, you might want to rethink your way of reaching the people.

Organizing public meetings. It is easy to plan public meetings too vaguely. Who will take responsibility for renting the building? Is there adequate parking? Is the lighting good? What about heating and ventilation? What about folding chairs and songbooks?

Who is in charge of the public-address system? Is there one on location, or must you supply one? Will someone record the sermons and supply interested people with tapes?

Who will take charge of having literature on display? Who

Chapter 4

will welcome visitors at the door? Will you have the visitors write their names and addresses for future contacts?

Who is in charge of the food? What facilities are on site for preparing it? What are you going to eat with, and where will you sit to eat?

Who will coordinate the lodging of overnight visitors?

Some of these questions you can answer on short notice. Others you should ask weeks ahead of time. Cooks in particular feel uncomfortable placed in charge of the food just a few days before the event.

Summer Bible school. Summer Bible school was once held up as a way of reaching out to people and giving children good memories to take with them through life. Today it has less impact because other activities compete (sports, amusements, and other churches' summer Bible schools).

This does not mean we should automatically throw out summer Bible school. Maybe in our locality it is still a good way of reaching the community, or maybe we simply want to have it for the benefit of our own church people. Neither should we keep a thing just because it has always been done.

One problem arises if we reach out only to children. Once they are about sixteen, they are too often gone. It is much more desirable to reach out to families. "If the lambs come, the sheep will follow" is a very weak argument, and it should be the other way around.

Homeschool conventions. Some people have serious reservations about getting involved at homeschool conventions. Several of their concerns are these: (1) If their church would not allow its own members to homeschool because of concerns about individualism, why should they capitalize on homeschooling as a way of reaching out to people, only to try to wean them away from it if they become church members? (2) Homeschool conventions have side features quite unlike what we approve of in church life. They have seminars in which

Reaching the Community

women teach men, for instance. Paying fees to the convention is an indirect way of supporting such.

There could be other concerns as well. Presently, however, a number of conservative people are doing business at homeschool conventions nationwide. They claim to be reaching people who would not otherwise be reached and even winning members this way. They would say the benefits seem to outweigh the problems.

See how your own church leaders feel about conventions. Some churches might want to sponsor the work and even appoint a committee directing it. Others might prefer to let individuals move ahead cautiously until it becomes clear whether the church should encourage or discourage the work. Still others might want you to stay away from conventions altogether and reach out to people in some other way.

If you work at a homeschool convention, here are some suggestions.

1. Frankly tell your publisher what you are doing. Publisher employees are in touch with other convention attendees and can give you valuable direction and advice. They can also help keep you from overlapping the efforts of others.

2. Send in a reservation form and down payment to the convention directors as soon as you can. Probably you will have to pay for each ten-foot space you want, tables if you want them, and an electrical outlet if you want that.

3. Honor personal checks. Most homeschoolers are decent people, and their checks probably will not bounce.

4. Honor credit cards if you can. Maybe you have a home business that is set up for credit cards, and all you need to do is bring your setup to the convention. One brother who does this says he figures about 30 percent of his sales are through Visa. A good portion of the people who use the card would not have been able to buy without it. This does not help him much financially, because as a businessman he has to pay 4 percent

Chapter 4

of his sales to the credit card company. His homeschool ventures are not much of a paying proposition anyway after he pays several hundred dollars just to get a place at the convention. He philosophizes that not many mission outreaches are paying propositions. He does it to reach people, not to make money.

By the way, between conventions, this brother stays available to take orders and ship books. Some people prefer to go through him, rather than directly to the publisher. One reason for this is that he will accept their checks more readily than the publisher does.

5. Try to have an experienced and outgoing lower-grade teacher with you to answer people's questions about curriculum.

6. Have some way of recording your transactions, whether by computer and printer, cash register, or sales slip pad.

7. Display free sermon tapes (preferably evaluated first; a good title does not necessarily make a good sermon.) People are most interested in tapes on the home, on women's place, on nonresistance, and on feet washing; they are curious about the distinctive doctrines. Have a church address on the tapes.

8. Display free tracts—some on education and maybe some on the distinctive doctrines.

9. Have an extension cord, a cash box, cash (counted) for change, bags for customer purchases, display racks, and a pocket calculator.

10. Order books in plenty of time. It takes several weeks to get them to you, and you might want to put price tags on them. (A word of warning: price stickers come off some books nicely but NOT others. You can easily turn a good book into a second if not careful.)

11. Get advice on how many to order of (1) most storybooks, (2) coloring/preschool books, (3) lower-level curriculum. Record books and plan books sell well. Upper-grade curriculum items do not sell as well.

12. For the coloring/preschool books, see if you can use a revolving rack.

13. Encourage customers to pick up catalogs. Rod and Staff pays vendors a small amount for every one they distribute. Rod and Staff also offers free books about the same size as catalogs that show a wide sampling of actual lessons from the curriculum. This is an effective idea. Have plenty of each.

14. Customers want to see what is inside shrink-wrapped packs (e.g. art packets). Open a pack of each level and have each sample pack coil-bound. One local stationery store did an excellent job in half an hour for about a dollar apiece.

15. Some people will buy from you first thing. Others will drop in at your stand several times before they buy. Remember that you are not strictly a businessperson at the convention. You are there to meet people, to be friendly, to answer questions about the display or about your beliefs, and to put in a good word where you can.

16. If you meet interested people, try to keep up the friendship after the convention. You may want to consider having a Sunday service locally the same weekend as the convention and see who shows up.

Newspaper interviews. A local newspaper might call and ask to interview you. Should you let it happen?

Although we are not publicity seekers, publicity of this sort can be all right. You will probably say to the reporter first, "I'll talk to some others and get back to you." Some brethren have definite opinions on this subject. They will probably advise you to say, "Certainly you may interview us, with the understanding that we may see your final draft."

When the reporter says, "No, we don't do it that way," you can say, "Fine. But if you decide to let us look over the article and pictures, we will be happy to have an interview with you." Since the news personnel have their dry times when there is not much news and they still must produce a newspaper, they

CHAPTER 4

will probably agree. Do not forget to express appreciation for the privilege to review their work.

Church people have had good experiences with newspapers even without the stipulation that they must check the article. Reporters have even checked back voluntarily to make sure their facts were straight. However, there have been unpleasant moments too. So often reporters have preconceived ideas that find their way into print. Or they may highlight one point at the expense of proportion. One Utah newspaper declared that Mennonite men kiss the men and the women kiss the women on the lips at every service. Perfectly true, but the prominence the paper put on this issue gave an impure cast to the article.

Remember this though: people featured in a news article see it in a totally different light from those who casually read it. What might seem very embarrassing to us, a normal newspaper reader might pass over without a thought.

Be friendly and open with reporters. Consider having them for a meal. It is part of reaching out, and reaching out is why you are where you are.

Street services. This probably consists of singing and short talks along a street or in a park while several brethren talk to bystanders or hand out tracts.

Know the rules—and make sure everyone in the outreach remembers them. One outreach got permission from shopping center authorities to sing on the premises, with the stipulation that the group should not be handing out papers. After a time or two, the center authorities learned that some people were handing out papers after all. Somehow, the word had not gotten to everyone. The group lost their privilege.

Have a large stand-alone tract rack, where you put tracts on the distinctive doctrines and on practical subjects—for example, competitive sports, insurance, divorce and remarriage, the discipline of children, and so on. Keep the rack off to one side, out of the direct public eye. People look around to see if they are being watched before they slip a tract like *"So You Want to Stop Smoking?"* from the rack.

Coach the people who hand out tracts. A few eager ones may need to be advised not to hand out tracts about the Christian woman's veiling on the street. Others must be cautioned not to approach people too suddenly with a tract; people need a moment to think before they respond.

If questioned by people, you need not think you must have the answer to every question. However, you should at least be ready to say what Jesus means to you. "Be ready always to give an answer to every man that asketh you a reason of the hope that is in you" (1 Peter 3:15).

Do not interfere with town business. If you sing in a group, stand where the sidewalk will not be blocked and where people will not have to detour to get into a store. If a shopkeeper objects to what you are doing, go farther up the street.

Do not sing too fast. People tend to do so when excited or self-conscious. A strong leader who starts slowly and takes an extra moment between verses can help this.

Avoid staring at strange sights that pass; avoid smiling to each other about them. You are just as visible to city people as they are to you.

Let the joy of the Lord show, remembering the tendency many of us have to be sober-sided if self-conscious. Look reasonably pleasant. It is a way of talking people's language.

Tract racks. The following article is available in leaflet form from Rod and Staff Publishers.

Guidelines for Tract-Rack Evangelism

What Is Tract-Rack Evangelism? Tract-rack evangelism is effort put forth to distribute Gospel literature by placing and maintaining free-literature racks in public places. Does it really work? Do people have enough interest in Bible literature that they will stop and take a tract? The

CHAPTER 4

answer is an emphatic *yes.*

Why Is There a Need for Tract-Rack Evangelism? The spiritual temperature of too many churches is lukewarm or cold. This has brought on an increasing departure from Christian principles, and spiritual darkness is settling in. As a result, the world is greatly confused and does not understand what truth is or where it is found. Indulging in the sins of the flesh, they find only greater emptiness and anguish of heart. Many are asking, "Where is peace, where is satisfaction, and where is real meaning in life?"

Tract-rack evangelism is an effective way of getting sound Gospel literature into the hands of those seekers. They need to learn to know Jesus. He is the Light of the world and is the answer to the needs of the human heart (John 8:12). However, many seekers are not quite ready to openly admit that they have a need, and they will not open themselves to Christians (especially strangers) to have salvation explained. But when they are alone, standing in front of a tract rack, they may take some literature on a subject that interests them.

Placing tract racks in public places makes Bible teaching available to whoever wants it, without "pestering" those who have no interest. We can be relatively certain that tracts selected from a rack are in the hands of individuals who have a degree of spiritual interest. Also, the very presence of the rack in a place where people come regularly (such as a bank or a supermarket) serves as a continual reminder to those who are rejecting God. Its silent yet forceful message is that God's Word has the answers for the needs of humanity.

Reaching the Community

Where Should Tract Racks Be Installed? You can place tract racks in any public place where the management accepts them, and where you can service and refill them without marring your testimony or facing undue temptations. Just remember that when you reach out to a sinner in the depths of sin, you get very close to sin and its environment, so use care and pray lest you be led astray.

Some good places to install tract racks are family restaurants, barber shops, . . . laundromats, markets, airports, bus terminals, train stations, auction houses, factories, stores, garages (in the sitting and waiting area), hospitals, doctors' and dentists' offices, tourist attractions, campgrounds, and banks. Ask the Lord for direction in finding places where His Word will reach needy souls. *"Seek, and ye shall find."*

Installing Tract Racks. The best time to ask permission to install a rack is usually between 8:00 A.M. and 5:00 P.M., when the managers or owners are around. Clear it with the owner if possible, unless the manager can assure you that he has the authority to give you permission.

Show the owner or manager six or more colorful evangelistic tracts. If he asks if the tracts are denominational, tell him that you have some that are, but if he wishes, you will refrain from placing that kind there. If that is his desire, mark "No Denominational" at the top of your record sheet for that rack. Also, you should have your church name, and a minister's address and telephone number on the back of the tract for interested persons to contact.

Whenever possible, place the rack in an annex

Chapter 4

or an area where most people pass through, but where not everyone will see them pick up literature. At cash registers, people are busy paying their bills and putting away their wallets, so that is not a good place. Before they leave the building, they may pick up free announcements, sale bills, and so forth. That is the place for the Gospel tract rack to be placed too.

If the owners want to read some literature first and think about it, or check with others involved in the business, tell them you will check back in a week. Then be sure to check back promptly—but do not telephone: that makes it too easy for them to say no, and it shows less effort on your part.

Tell them that if any problem turns up with the literature, they can call the telephone number on the back of the literature to have the problem corrected, or the rack can be removed if they find that necessary. If they are in doubt about the placement, tell them to try it and you will check back in two weeks to see how it is working out.

Maintaining the Rack. After the rack has been placed, check it in three to five days to see how it has gained acceptance. Maybe someone other than the manager wanted it out of the way and has set it aside. If it is under a counter or in a closet, you should get it before it is thrown out.

Regular two-week checkups are the best. Even if the literature moves well, change to other tracts so that people can see that it is a freshly tended message center. This draws their attention. You can leave the same literature in a rack for four weeks, but no longer; and it should be

Reaching the Community

checked every two weeks or less, especially if you find it regularly messed up.

Keep a record book or sheet for each rack that you have installed. Record the title and the quantity of each tract that you have put in or have taken out of the rack. Also, record the date each time the rack was checked or changed.

By keeping good records, you can see at a glance which tracts move well and which move slowly. You also can rotate your tracts without repeating too quickly.

When other literature is placed in your rack (maybe because you needed help to fill it, or let it go too long), take it out and lay it somewhere. But do to this literature as you would have others do to yours, although the rack is yours.

Keep a good variety of literature in the rack. You should have some evangelistic tracts that explain the steps of repentance and salvation, and warn of judgment; you also should have some practical tracts on subjects like the home, immodesty, prayer, and the church. Display some tracts on current issues such as smoking, abortion, and humanism; also use some doctrinal tracts for the more mature seeker. It may be good to display a reply post card so that the seeker can request more material.

"Cast thy bread upon the waters: for thou shalt find it after many days" (Ecclesiastes 11:1).[1]

A few additional suggestions. Keep the tracts supplied from a central source for the congregation. This is more convenient

---

[1] Dennis Bennetch, "Guidelines for Tract-Rack Evangelism" (Crockett, KY: Rod and Staff Publishers).

CHAPTER 4

than each person buying his own tracts. One person should assume the number of racks he is comfortable with, for as long as he is comfortable. Six racks are workable and not too burdensome for one person.

As was already implied, the tracts should have the minister's name and/or the church name and telephone number so people can make contacts if they wish.

Show good taste. For example, keep rack displays from hitting one theme too hard. Rack patrons might be repelled by a display featuring (all at one time) *A Terrifying Thought*, *The Gates of Hell*, *When the World's on Fire*, and *You Are Dead a Long Time*.

Avoid filling the rack pockets altogether full; that gives the impression that no one is taking any.

Again, avoid misunderstandings, as a group in Oregon found out to their sorrow.

> One restaurant in Albany, Merl's Chuckwagon, allowed the rack in their lobby for a year or so. It was stocked with booklets on salvation and various doctrinal subjects. During the time the rack was in use, approximately $300.00 worth of booklets were taken monthly. Apparently there was a misunderstanding between the restaurant owner and those maintaining the rack. One day the proprietor's pastor from the Assembly of God church picked up a booklet on the dangers of the tongues movement and asked his parishioner why he had a booklet like that in his establishment. After looking at it, the owner asked the Mennonites to remove their literature. It was his understanding that literature would be directed only toward salvation themes and not doctrinal subjects.[2]

---

[2] Jason Schrock, *Lengthen the Cords, Strengthen the Stakes* (Tangent, Oregon: Tangent Mennonite Church History Committee, 2000), p. 173.

Reaching the Community

On a smaller scale, you might get permission simply to drop a few tracts or booklets now and then on waiting-room tables in doctor's offices and barbershops. Judging from the looks of the tables, people from other denominations are doing it. Why should not we do the same? Sometimes donating a child's storybook might be appropriate.

Foreign-language tracts. At the time of this writing, Rod and Staff offers a number of Spanish tracts, a few German ones, and one in French. Grace Press offers some Russian tracts. Lamp and Light has a major Spanish outreach, including quite a few Spanish tracts, and also a few tracts in French and German.

Retirement-home programs. Presenting programs in retirement homes may not be as much of a soul-winning venture, because most of the people there are past the commitment-making age. This does not mean that the programs are wrong, but the fruit will be less obvious.

If you present programs, keep a few principles in mind. Many elderly people retire early in the evening. A 7:30 P.M. meeting is already far too late for some of them. Starting at seven o'clock is a slight improvement. It might be the best that you can do, considering your own people's schedules.

Make the devotional time either short or punchy, preferably both. Five minutes is long enough. A long, droning lecture will quickly shrink the number of residents who attend the next time.

Meet and talk to the residents afterwards, and make sure your children do too. You might want to sit down beside an elderly person and chat for a while.

Despite the pessimistic note this section began on, salvation themes are not out of place. They might stir a sinner or encourage some quiet resident (or staff member) who does already love the Lord. You never know.

Handing out monthly papers. In some communities, churches find it disappointing to knock at people's doors. One

CHAPTER 4

brother remarked, "The only ones who let us in were the ones who wanted to talk to *us.*" The ones they were trying to reach did not want to talk. Furthermore, if they knocked, they got quite a few refusals. Some people even said, "We don't want your papers anymore."

What they then do is drop off papers without knocking. If it is an area they only cover once a quarter, they leave a reply card. For them, that is more satisfactory.

Other churches encourage people to knock and say a few words, especially if the property resident knows a caller is there. The church might also leave it open to individuals, whatever they are comfortable with. Single women should go in pairs, and they might prefer not to knock.

Monthly papers tend to suffer in quality a bit, simply because they must come out so frequently that writers cannot put all the thought into them they would ordinarily put into a tract. There may be months when you slip a good tract into each paper.

Sometimes go to an area you have never covered before. If you hand out papers at the same area once a month, some people will think you come around every Sunday.

Two good monthly papers are *The Star of Hope,* issued by Rod and Staff Publishers, and *Living Waters,* from Eastern Mennonite Publications.

Recorded tapes. A tape ministry is especially good in relating to homeschoolers and others who live far from our churches. Mail them free sermon tapes about twice a month. The church might want to subsidize this.

Even this system, good as it is, needs follow-up. Sometimes it is good to travel to an area where several outlying families live and bring them together for services.

Tapes are good for reaching people close by too. In some cases you can perpetuate a contact by giving a tape and saying, "May I come back in a month to pick it up?"

Reaching the Community

Somehow, tapes give people a feel for what is happening in our church that is different from what they get by reading. Sometimes the information they get is more satisfying too. In one situation a brother has about forty standard tapes, making up what are called the "Honest Answers" list. Too many people were saying, "We can't get honest answers to our questions!" From time to time new tapes are added, and some that are not in demand are taken off. Several times a year, order blanks are sent out with updated lists. A dollar a tape to cover expenses is suggested; however, there is no obligation. On the back of the tape list, is a list of articles and information people can order. "Guidelines for Training Young Children" sells for three dollars to people who can afford it.

Prison ministries. *One writer made the following observations:*

> In America today there is an ever-growing prison population. The question could be raised: How can we meet the spiritual needs of these people? We remember the words of Jesus "I was in prison, and ye came unto me" (Matthew 25:36).
>
> The prison ministry presents some unique opportunities. For one thing, inmates have time on their hands. Therefore it is possible to visit with people who may have been too busy to talk about spiritual matters before. Also a prison sentence may jolt a person enough to cause him to reevaluate his priorities and goals for life. Thirdly, a sense of guilt and personal failure may cause a prisoner to sense his need of the Savior.
>
> Generally, the prison is not the place for heavy theological discourses. More than likely your audience will not be well versed in Bible doctrines. Basic Bible themes should be the backbone of our prison ministry.
>
> Spiritual instruction is not always well received

CHAPTER 4

by prisoners. Sometimes they are indifferent. And occasionally they snicker. In these situations remember the words of the Lord in Jeremiah 1:8, "Be not afraid of their faces." Courageously present the Word in faith that it will not return void.

When interest among prisoners is at a low ebb, you may use Bible stories as the basis for your study in order to generate interest. And if the jail permits, bring a group from church for a service. This is a good time to include young people. The prisoners enjoy the singing, and the service strengthens the impact of the regular Bible study sessions.[3]

Not only visiting but also writing to prisoners may be valuable:

When prison inmates have an awakening experience through reading the Scriptures, quite often they express a desire to have a Christian pen pal. They want someone with whom to test their thinking, and to ask questions about seemingly difficult passages or about their own personal struggles. Their hearts ache for answers to many, many questions. They occasionally write to publishers of Christian literature, and sometimes send letters to editors of local newspapers asking for Christian pen pals.

If these contacts are within reach, it is good to follow up with one-to-one visits. Personal visiting enables you to learn to know the inmate[s] better than by writing. It also assures them that you are truly interested in their spiritual life. Many prisoners have expressed a deep appreciation for

---

[3] Gerald Burkholder, "Church Committee Report: Prison Visitation," *The Eastern Mennonite Testimony,* September 1999, pp. 9, 7.

those who were willing to spend t me discussing the Scriptures and praying with them.[4]

A few other observations:

1. A prison for youth might have a mentoring program. In such a program, the prison welcomes a man who will befriend one or even more than one prisoner. He spends time with the prisoner, mainly just talking. A mentor should expect some difficulty finding time on the prison schedule, since prisons for youth keep the prisoners busy.

2. Remember that many times prisoners become very religious. Thousands of prisoners have enrolled in Lamp and Light Bible courses. Many of them have responded to the Gospel message. However, it is hard to know what becomes of them once they hit the street again. There should be follow-up. Lamp and Light does refer many prisoners to local churches.

3. Think twice about bringing women into men's prisons. Women understandably do not like to be stared at the way some prisoners do it. Do not assume that every prisoner had a good mother. She might be in the women's prison.

4. Some prisons are already overwhelmed with churches wanting to minister to the prisoners. It seems sensible to frequent those prisons that have more openings, or to find some other ministry entirely. Maybe you can reach people before they go to prison.

Gospel signs. The book *A Sower Went Forth*[5] tells of how Ralph Palmer caught the vision to put up Gospel signs. The signs said things like "Jesus Saves," "Christ Is the Answer," "Obey God's Word," "Eternity Ahead," and "Repent Now!" More recently, there has been a popular movement to have Gospel

---

[4] James J. Martin, "Prison Evangelism," *The Eastern Mennonite Testimony,* September 1992, p. 9.

[5] Martha Shenk Palmer, *A Sower Went Forth,* (Crockett, KY: Rod and Staff Publishers, 1978).

Chapter 4

signposts in front of people's homes. These are designed so that the message can be changed from time to time and keep catching the eyes of passersby.

A report in 1997 said this:

> Approximately ten years ago, a group of brethren began exchanging Gospel sign messages in an effort to remind people of God and His Word. Today, there are at least 1,300 different Gospel sign messages in circulation throughout the States and in foreign countries. The largest percent are in the English language; however, a few have been made in Spanish for Spanish-speaking countries.
>
> The Gospel sign work is done on a volunteer basis. Voluntary service personnel rotate signs from one place to another once a month. Signs[6] need to be lettered and decorated; signposts need to be made. Damages need to be repaired, and the irreparable posts need to be replaced. We see these as opportunities for those who are interested in VS service. . . .
>
> Following are a few messages which have drawn responses from those passing by. "There Are No Tears in Heaven" (Revelation 21:4). A woman whose mother had passed away said, "You don't know how often I read your sign. It has meant so much to me." "Wine Is a Mocker" (Proverbs 20:1). "Upon hearing a noise at the Gospel sign," one brother commented, "I went out to see what was happening. A liquor bottle was lying on the ground below the sign."

---

[6] A good size for such a sign is approximately 20" x 24". Some signposts include a mailbox holder.

Reaching the Community

Apparently the message was read, the Holy Spirit was at work.[7]

To be effective, a sign must look as if someone cares about it. Once a brother was embarrassed when traveling with some friends who noticed a sign of his on the edge of a field. Grass had grown up around it, so they stopped and cleared it away with their hands. The brother responsible for the sign helped too and held his peace, but he learned a lesson that day.

Scrapbooks. Lives have been touched by scrapbooks that would not have been touched by any other means. Scrapbooks are rarely refused, and often those who receive them send thank-you notes to the congregation who put the scrapbooks together.

However, small outreaches do not have enough people to make a scrapbook unless each family makes half a dozen pages—a discouraging prospect! In this case, they might call on the people back home now and then, describing someone's need and letting the home people make most of the pages. One caution: not only the people in outreach but also the people back home can be very busy and should not be overwhelmed with too many scrapbook-page assignments.

Cottage meetings. Many of us have good memories of cottage meetings, memories that go back to childhood. But there might be bad memories too, not only for us but also for people who opened their homes for the meetings. Here is some advice on the subject.

> The term "cottage meeting" was coined during an era of intensive home mission work in the past. It reflects an interest in reaching out to the needy in their homes. Individuals who are responsible to plan these efforts face several questions.

---

7 Aaron S. Hurst, "Gospel Signs," *The Eastern Mennonite Testimony,* July 1997, pp. 8, 9.

CHAPTER 4

1. Where should we go for cottage meetings? One responsibility of the church is to provide for her own. A cottage meeting can provide stimulating fellowship for members who have been unable to attend worship services due to age or illness. We should not overlook these brethren and sisters.

A cottage meeting can be a means of reaching out to the lost in the community. There are those who are open to such a contact. Others will not be open. We need to be discerning and approach those who would have some interest. Elderly folks whose social life is somewhat limited often are more willing to open their homes for a cottage meeting, but we need to look for others as well. Is there someone suffering from accident or illness whose heart may be more open at such a time? Is there someone who has shown interest by discussing spiritual things, or who has requested prayer? Such situations are excellent possibilities for cottage meetings. Contacts through personal visits or literature distribution may also open the door for a cottage meeting.

2. How should we arrange for cottage meetings? Go in person to ask permission for a cottage meeting—a telephone call is less personal and more easily shrugged off. A letter may be left unanswered. Appropriate appearance, friendliness, and courtesy go a long way in encouraging an individual to accept a cottage meeting visit.

The cottage meeting should not be a series of unsettling surprises for the hosts. Therefore, you should mention the approximate number of people who will attend. Often the group cannot be a very large one. Many congregations divide

Reaching the Community

into several groups for this purpose, contacting a number of homes at one time. If the group is to sit for the meeting, assure the hosts that you will provide and set up the chairs. If the hosts are unfamiliar with our services, give some description of what the meeting will be like. When you receive permission to hold a cottage meeting, leave your name and telephone number so that they can contact you if they would need to change their plans.

3. *What are some practical pointers for cottage meetings?* Groups sometimes meet at the church before going to the home where the meeting is to be. If this is done, be realistic in calculating the amount of time required for gathering and then traveling to the home. Plan the meeting with your hosts accordingly, and then be on time. Be aware if parking space is limited and have a plan to avoid confusion.

Be orderly in entering the home. Have you planned a place for coats and hats if necessary? Someone also needs to be responsible to see that chairs and songbooks are along and put in place. [Sometimes it is appropriate to stand for a short service.]

The group should include someone whom the hosts know, possibly the person who made the contact. It may be well for this person to be the moderator of the meeting, or at least to introduce the moderator to the hosts.

A cottage meeting service often consists mostly of singing. Those who plan the arrangement of the groups should consider the singing abilities of the families as they make those

CHAPTER 4

arrangements. Appropriate songs must be chosen to fit the needs of the various individuals to whom you will minister. Elderly people may especially appreciate the old, familiar hymns. Some situations call for hymns containing specific spiritual challenges.

The Scripture passage for the devotional period also needs to be carefully chosen, considering the needs and the level of spiritual understanding of the hosts. If possible, it is good to follow the devotional period with a song relating to the devotional theme. Sometime during the service, you should give the hosts opportunity to choose a song they would like to have sung. Provide a songbook so they can participate, or at least follow the words and better appreciate the messages of the songs. A song about heaven can provide a good note on which to close.

Length of the service may vary, depending on the physical condition of the hosts, but generally, the service should not be more than an hour. Refrain from lengthy visits among yourselves after the service, but rather be ready to share a few friendly or encouraging words with your hosts. Orderliness must be the rule in our departure as well as when we arrive and when we worship.

God can use the careful planning and sincere efforts of the congregation to touch the hearts of needy persons through the ministry of cottage meetings. This work is worthy of our faithful support.[8]

Remember to follow up with personal visits.

---

[8] Rodney L. Sensenig, Sr., "Congregational Outreach Work—Cottage Meetings," *The Eastern Mennonite Testimony,* October 1993, pp. 9, 10.

Reaching the Community

Disaster aid. On February of 1991, the *Seattle Post-Intelligencer* ran an article about volunteer workers who helped to clean up after flooding.

> "For six straight weeks, crews of Mennonite volunteers have fanned out across Fir Island, going from home to farm, performing what residents have come to consider miracle work. In the aftermath of a disaster—and also in a time of war—the Mennonites' living demonstration of the Golden Rule carries added weight. They seem an anomaly in this age of hype, shunning publicity if at all possible, living non-violent, humble lives and aiding Mennonite and non-Mennonite alike."9

Ethical questions do arise. After Hurricane Agnes devastated areas along the Susquehanna River in 1972, relief workers moved in to clean up people's basements. Men slogged in and out, carrying muddy, soaked objects that discouraged owners wanted to dump. Mennonites who had been brought up to "waste not, want not" regretted to see these items thrown away and often made arrangements with the owners to take them home. Afterwards the church recommended that the new owners of the salvaged items make contact with the previous owners and pay them for what they had taken. It left a better testimony.

Modern-day complications can hamper a relief worker. After a windstorm caused damage in central Pennsylvania, a group of workers went to help clean up. Property owner after property owner held them off with the same story. They were waiting for the insurance man to show up and appraise the damage

---

9 John Marshall, "Hope and Charity on Fir Island," *Seattle Post-Intelligencer,* February 20, 1991, quoted in Jason Schrock's, *Lengthen the Cords; Strengthen the Stakes* (Tangent Mennonite Church History Committee), c. 2000, pp. 248, 249.

CHAPTER 4

before the cleanup began. It was hard to find work to do, and one brother remarked, "By the end of that day, I was tired."

Recognizing the problem is one thing; knowing what to do about it is another. Perhaps the group should have sent a brother or two ahead the previous day to get a truer picture of the needs.

Activities for the young. A number of useful outreach projects can involve young people. However, these same projects can involve people of other ages too, and usually they should. Segregating young people from other ages for special activities can be counterproductive. High-spirited young people can create an overly light atmosphere among themselves that would not develop among a mixed age group.

Above all, a play mentality may develop. For one illustration, a youth group got together to have a Bible study and end with a little volleyball. A year later they were having a little Bible study and a lot of volleyball. Young people should be developing a service mentality and an outreach vision. We want them to be adults, rather than being adolescents for ten or fifteen years.

There is a place for getting together to address tracts, clean up someone's garden, and so on. However, in many cases, things can be done on a family or church basis.

Helpful periodicals. Here are gleanings from an article called "Maintaining Contact."

> With winter fast approaching, summertime evangelistic activities, street meetings, and passing out tracts give way to other demanding activities such as Regional Bible School. With this shift of schedules, what happens with the folks who showed a definite interest in the Gospel this summer through street meetings? What about that tourist you met who expressed interest in your faith? How can we lead an interested business customer to a fuller knowledge of the truth? In the midst of busy schedules, how do

Reaching the Community

we keep in contact with those who seem to be searching? . . .

In answer to this question, the vision for the periodical *Light of Life* was born. . . .

It is a sixteen-page booklet, published quarterly by Rod and Staff, with some doctrinal articles written on a fairly elementary level. It is designed to increase Bible knowledge, to expose the reader to practical Christian experience and discipleship, and to stimulate personal study of the Scriptures. To illustrate this, the titles of one issue of *Light of Life* were as follows: "Is It Hard to Love an Enemy?" "The Christian's Love for God's Word," "It Is Time Your Luck Ran Out," and "The Evidence for Creation." Each issue carries an article on the home as well as several stories for the family. Practically all the articles and stories are an assortment from various Rod and Staff periodicals.

How does the mailing system work? Individualized labeling is too cumbersome and expensive for the publisher. To make this periodical serve best, a bulk mailing is received by one of our brethren who is in charge of the mailing list. Volunteer help is used to place address labels and to sort for mailing. Inside each cover is a label that identifies who sponsors this paper. It may be a congregation or an individua . This label may read something like this: "This periodical is given for your spiritual inspiration. Courtesy of the Mountain Ridge Mennonite Church." An address and phone number is also included. . . .

This paper has been a blessing to many. Several months ago while shopping, a sponsor heard

Chapter 4

from behind him, "Sir, I'd like to thank you for the paper you send. I look forward to receiving it every quarter. Each time I receive it, I cannot help thinking about what you stand for." [10]

The *Light of Life* has German and Spanish editions named, respectively, *Licht des Lebens* and *Luz de la vida*. These monthly periodicals have thirty-two pages rather than sixteen. *Licht des Lebens*, according to the Rod and Staff catalog, is "for the whole family—from preschool to adult. It includes stories, articles, and illustrations and is designed to present clear Bible teachings sometimes overlooked or neglected by modern-day Christendom."

Reaching Out is another attractive paper, self-described as follows. "A quarterly magazine designed to assist in witnessing in communities served by conservative Mennonite churches. The magazine targets the lost as well as professing Christians around us. Churches and individuals use it in a variety of ways including mailings, personal distribution, and street witnessing." Contact *Reaching Out,* P.O. Box 555, Seymour, MO 65746.

Other ways. Churches have found a variety of interesting ways to reach out to people. Following are some things churches have done.

Place children's books and doctrinal books free of charge in a local library. The library allows their church name and telephone number in the books. How many people read the books while in the library, no one knows, but the books have been checked out rather frequently. Rod and Staff has seen the value of this. Recently they sent out a letter saying, "Some brethren across the United States and Canada have donated Rod and Staff books to public libraries. We believe this has been effective in touching lives. We would like to make it easier for others to enter into these efforts. Following are four

---

[10] Wayne Rudolph, "Church Committee Report: Maintaining Contact," *The Eastern Mennonite Testimony,* October 1999, pp. 8, 9.

different packages we are offering." The smallest package is a set of five books: *Young Man, Be Strong; Dear Princess; Ye Fathers; The Christian Home;* and *A Time to Plant.*

Place Rod and Staff's Little Jewel books in waiting rooms of doctors, dentists, chiropractors, and veterinarians. Often such rooms have a child's corner especially suited to this. The doctors appreciate it. Evidently the clients do too—the books keep disappearing!

Some have the name and telephone number of their church in the yellow pages. Congregations have members now who made contact first of all through the telephone book.

Some have free-tape dispensers built on the side of their tract racks. The tapes move, so evidently some people are interested.

Many groups visit local hospitals. They sing in halls or go from room to room singing and perhaps having a short Scripture reading.

Other ideas that may be helpful:

1. Have church cards giving information about service times. Have a simple map on the card directing people to the church. Members can carry them in their business vehicles and give them to anyone interested.

2. Consider putting into local papers short articles teaching Bible truth about issues of interest.

3. Set up a display of Christian literature in a flea market or other public place.

4. Have a last-day-of-school program and invite friends and neighbors, including those who normally do not come to church services.

Nearby cities. During the 1900s, there was a big push among Mennonites to start missions in the cities. These missions were tried, but by now they have moved far from the original vision and no longer maintain Scriptural standards. Conservative Mennonites understandably are not too eager to try again.

Chapter 4

What then—shall we leave the cities strictly alone? Maybe we should set up homes and churches nearby and do our shopping and other business in the city. Then we can draw interested people out. This will be safer for us and better for them. Admittedly, living in the suburbs is expensive, but it is worth considering. One example of this might be the congregation at Mendon, Massachusetts, about an hour's drive from Boston.

If we are too far away from the city we are trying to reach, and not prepared to move closer, we probably will have little to show for our efforts. There is little fruit in hit-and-run evangelism.

Weddings and funerals: People who would not attend any other service do come to weddings and funerals. This is an opportunity for some gentle evangelism. The experience of an Ontario minister of a generation past illustrates this.

> He had the privilege of preaching at the funeral service of a local man, reputed to be a boozer. So he began, "(He) and I had one thing in common: we both loved flowers." Then he went on to challenge the congregation with the claims of the Gospel in the face of life's uncertainty.
>
> Another time he was called to preach at the funeral of a man known as the town eccentric. He reported, "There was present that day the greatest collection of non-Christians and unchurched that I had ever had before me. So I preached the Word—'There is none other name under heaven given among men, whereby we must be saved.' " The next day someone called and said, "You preached against Mary." The minister replied, "No, I preached Christ, and everything I said was in the Word of God!"[11]

---

[11] Urie Bender, *Four Earthen Vessels* (Kitchener, Ont.: Herald Press, 1982), p. 102.

Reaching the Community

People learn more about the Gospel if they are comfortable at the service and do not have too many distractions. Kneeling for prayer might surprise them; the devotional leader or moderator should clearly announce this practice beforehand.

Being friendly at a wedding reception or at a graveside can touch people as much as anything that is said during the service. Sometimes merely standing beside a grieving person at the graveside is the best thing you can do.

Personal Contacts

"There cometh a woman of Samaria to draw water: Jesus saith unto her, Give me to drink."
John 4:7

Which are more important—personal contacts on a one-to-one basis or church-sponsored outreach activities? Each needs the other, of course. Without church-sponsored activities to keep the vision alive, we would probably end up with fewer people making personal contacts. However, church activities are not complete without individuals talking to individuals. Not many contacts surpass the one made over the garden fence.

Visiting people. Sometimes people seek us; other times we must seek them. It would be a mistake to always "wait on the Lord" if He has in mind things we can do. In fact, when a fruitful contact is made, both sides must be doing some seeking. One man who contacted a pastor would have liked to pay a visit, but his wife was not well. The pastor took it on himself to ask if he should come and visit them. This worked out nicely for both sides.

Visit the invalids and the ill, if they are not *too* ill. Respect hospital limitations on visiting, and impose limits on yourself without being told.

When visiting an ungodly person in the hospital, try not to make him feel trapped. A carnation as a simple gesture of

CHAPTER 4

goodwill might open his heart to the message of the Gospel more than many words could do.

Get-well cards have their place. But one brother remembers a hospital experience during his youth when he received a card from a ladies' Sunday school class. The sender was the secretary of the class, and the card contained a neatly typed list of all the members in the class, most of whom he did not know. Perhaps it was better than nothing, but it struck him as being rather cold.

Visit old people. What seems like a fleeting day to us can seem as long as a week to people who sit in the quiet with nothing much to do. Visit people who want to talk. Some of them are quite interesting, and from the less interesting ones, you still can probably learn. If they often repeat their stories, remember that it seems God has programed elderly people to repeat their stories for emphasis before they are gone.

Visit people who invite you to come. What more do you want than an invitation? If someone says, "Why don't you come over for coffee?" take him seriously. You may or may not care for coffee, but you care for people.

A brother remembers having car trouble along the highway. Someone stopped to help, spending a fair amount of time getting acquainted in the process. When the problems were fixed, his benefactor said, "Now, you're coming to our home for supper!" The brother had spent so much downtime already that he was in a hurry. He talked himself out of the invitation. Afterwards he was sorry and wished he had spent more time with his newfound friend.

Visit those having problems. A few might not want to talk about their problems and only want the genial company of friends. Others want to talk about their problems, even if not when you first walk in the door.

A young woman visited a close friend whose brother had died in a car accident. Trying to show good taste, she talked

Reaching the Community

about every subject but the one heaviest on both of their minds, only to learn afterwards that her friend had been aching to talk about her brother. The lesson: do not disappoint people by skirting the subject. Send out a "diplomatic feeler," and see what they do with it.

Be considerate. Not everyone is used to big families. Have the children be reasonably quiet and pick up their toys when they leave. It is also appropriate for children just to sit quietly and listen to older people. Remember to leave soon enough.

What to say when visiting. For some people, "What can you say?" is an amusingly unnecessary question. However, if you desire some ideas for what to say, here are a few ideas:

1. You might ask the host how he met his wife (but only if you know that their marriage is intact), and tell how you met yours. Ask what he does when he has free time. Ask if he read any books lately or if he would rather be busy with his hands. Ask if he does any gardening.

2. Often you do not need to ask questions at all. Tell a few family stories; it is all right to let it slip that you have your human side. Talk about an answered prayer you had recently. Sing some old familiar hymns if the people you are visiting are so inclined. In some homes you are welcome to read the Bible.

3. Try not to put pressure on people. One brother says, "I am guided a lot by the questions they ask, and the areas they show interest in. It is interesting how the Holy Spirit can use such a course and get you into areas that were necessary to discuss."

4. If they ask about the distinctive doctrines, tell them. If not, avoid confronting them with such matters until you have established a relationship. If they claim to be Christians, you might ask, "When did you give your heart to the Lord?" Then do not pour cold water on their testimony, considering the example of the Lord: "A bruised reed shall he not break, and the smoking flax shall he not quench" (Isaiah 42:3). Any little

Chapter 4

evidence of faith we should encourage, even if it does have a long way to go.

5. Keep the ratio right. One young man became frustrated when he invited more than one neighboring family for a meal. They outnumbered him and set the tone for the occasion simply by talking the way they usually talked. He had trouble getting the conversation onto a higher level.

6. When company comes to your home, do not apologize for the looks of your house or your simple meal. Your company might live in even humbler state than you, and your apologies could make them uneasy.

7. You can make friends by asking for advice or a favor. Jesus did. "Give me to drink," He said to the woman at Jacob's well, and a profitable conversation went on from there.

8. Go to your neighbor and say, "We found this plant growing in the flower bed. Do you have any idea what it is?" Get a neighbor to come over and shoot your pestiferous groundhog. Ask him to help when your battery has gone dead. One neighbor not only helped get a van started but also took the occasion to offer the use of his garden tiller, any time, free of charge.

9. If you ask a small favor, do not offer to pay for it, as that cheapens what they have done for you. A bigger favor, like borrowing someone's garden tiller, might call for reimbursement. Naturally, you would refill the gas tank. Maybe sometime you can drop off a gift of freshly baked buns.

10. If a neighbor drops in and asks you to come and see a wild lady's slipper growing in his yard, by all means go and admire it. If someone pulls into the driveway across the street with a deer in the back of his pickup, you might want to stroll over and make your comments.

11. Oh, yes, if you are leaving after a pleasant evening with friends, it is friendly to wave and toot the horn as you are going out the driveway. If they are visiting you, remember to stand outside as they leave, to see them off. Some people do all these

things by nature; others need to be prompted.

12. Should you give a tract to a neighbor during a social visit? Somehow, that seems a bit confrontative unless it addresses a subject about which you have been talking. A gift of a book or a tape recording of singing might be in order.

Social dangers. Do you feel that you are being pulled into a relationship that is not good for you and the children? Of course, you can socialize too much with unsaved neighbors. However, if you do your part in discussing the things of the Lord, that question will soon take care of itself.

Avoid being too pleased by people's compliments. Maybe a simple change of subject can help. Nicodemus said, "Rabbi, we know that thou art a teacher come from God: for no man can do these miracles that thou doest, except God be with him." Jesus brushed all this aside and came right to the point: "Except a man be born again, he cannot see the kingdom of God" (John 3:2, 3).

Perhaps someone says, "I sure am glad to have people from your church around for neighbors. Always so honest, so helpful . . ." It may be appropriate to say, "It's because of our relationship with the Lord. Do you know what it means to be born again?"

E-mail. The communication world is so much in flux these days that perhaps anything we say here will be out-of-date in a few years. But a few cautions in connection with e-mail are worth mentioning.

E-mail gives people the power to do a great deal of good—or a great deal of evil. Through it, a brother or sister can keep in touch with many seeking souls and give them considerable encouragement. Someone who is a little "off balance" can also spread his poison, sending it to a hundred people at once with the push of a button.

An e-mail circle can form a fellowship closer than the fellowship one finds at church. At least it can feel closer; it is easy

Chapter 4

to feel brotherly to someone you cannot see. E-mail could be robbing one's own church of loyalty it deserves and cannot do without.

Churches are putting curbs on the use of e-mail, and they deserve our respect for addressing the issue before the problem gets out of hand.

Talking people's language. The apostle Paul, trying to reach his fellow Jews, used the synagogue. As usual when visitors were present, the rulers of the synagogue gave him an opportunity to speak—and he did speak (Acts 13:15). He used Old Testament history as a way to introduce Jesus because he knew the Jews were familiar with this.

However, in Athens he used a different approach. Here he spoke to the people about their "UNKNOWN GOD." He quoted their poets. Since they were not very familiar with the Old Testament, he did not quote from it. Instead, he pressed God's claim on them on the basis that God had created them. He led up to Jesus Christ, just as he had when he spoke to the Jews, but by a different route.

How do you speak the children's language during the first few minutes of vacation Bible school, where children off the street are excited and talking and making noise? Some people would say, "We're glad to see all who have come out tonight and trust this will be a time of mutual blessing to everyone present. Brother Fred will lead us in two numbers of song, and then Brother John will conduct our devotional meditation." Can we do better than that? Why not just get up and say, "Let's sing!"

The same principle applies to one-on-one contacts. A missionary once visited a friend who said, "Well, what wind blows you here?" The missionary replied simply, "Well, the Lord whom I serve is interested in you and cares for you personally; He made me aware of this during the night, and I just thought I'd drop over to tell you this. We know each other professionally, but I don't believe that I have ever told you this other."[12] How is that for a simple opening?

You never speak people's language better than when things go wrong. They watch to see how you respond. Stephen never had a better pulpit than when he was tried before the Sanhedrin and finally stoned (Acts 7). And you never have a better one than when you drop a jar of pickles in the supermarket aisle, or come up five dollars short at the checkout, or have to track down someone whose car you dented. Yes, even one's own mistakes can serve the Lord's purposes.

Small gestures can do more than you might have expected:

> A nurse in a big city hospital once told of a patient, a skid-row derelict, who often said of a certain doctor, "He's the best doctor here, the best doctor in the whole hospital."
>
> The nurse was intrigued by his comment and wondered what professional actions or attitudes had given the man such a high opinion of the doctor.
>
> "What makes him so great?" she asked.
>
> "Every time he passes my bed, he tweaks my toe," was the unexpected reply.[13]

The children's contacts. The more interests your children have, the more people they will be able to relate to. If your child wants an aquarium or a parakeet, the idea is worth considering for that reason.

It is best not to overburden our children with the idea that they must be an "example" to others. Encourage them to

---

12 David A. Shank, *Who Will Answer?* (Scottdale, Pa.: Herald Press, 1969), p. 18.

13 Joe Bayly, "Compassion or Pity," Eternity (March 1969), p. 41, cited in David Augsburger's, *Witness Is Withness* (Chicago: Moody Press, 1971), pp. 53, 54.

Chapter 4

befriend the children of families to whom we relate. In addition, they should behave as well with others as we normally expect them to do at home.

Personal tract ministry. It is good to have a few tracts handy in a purse or pocket or glove compartment. Handing a person a tract, you might say, "I love the Lord, and I like to put in a good word for Him where I can." Or, you might remark that good things are for sharing, so you thought you would share this. Or, depending on the tract, you might say, "This is a universal problem; no matter who you give this to, it fits!" Or, "This message meant something to me, and maybe you'll find it that way too."

Naturally, be discreet. You would not put *The Mennonites* at a public telephone for whoever picks it up. You might even think twice before giving, *Neglected, Rejected, and Forgotten Truths* to a person interested in spiritual things. He could find it too much to swallow all at once. Try a simpler tract.

One brother who came into the Mennonite church said in effect: "God dealt with us on one issue at a time. If He had spoken to me first on the issue of nonresistance, I might not have listened."

Leading people to the Lord. Could it be that an otherwise well-run work breaks down at the point of actually communicating Christ to people? We have our programs and we have our papers, but bringing people face to face with Jesus Christ—there is the challenge.

This challenge is not something we can brush off on other people. You might be the only person standing at another person's crossroad. If you doubt that, read the testimonies of people who got right with God. Often after they describe how far from God they were, they will say, "But I met someone . . ."

To reach someone for the Lord, be tactful, be pleasant. However, do not be so tactful you do not get anything said. Pretend you are selling the other person your car. You have to

Reaching the Community

speak plainly enough to get across your point.

Do not assume that people know what you know. One man helping a friend find his way into the Bible mentioned a certain chapter, and his friend said vaguely, "Chapter, chapter . . ." He did not know what a chapter was. Another man, on being asked if he was born again, replied, "I've never been baptized, if that's what you mean." By worldly standards, he was far from ignorant, having once been a test pilot and then a real estate salesman. Nevertheless, on this point he knew little.

What should you say to lead a person to the Lord? Well, the person to whom you are speaking, if lost, should realize he *is* lost. However, that is a rather negative way to start. Many soul winners prefer to start with the thought that "God loves you and has a wonderful plan for your life." They support this with John 3:16 and with John 10:10, which says, "I am come that they might have life, and that they might have it more abundantly." Then they move into the following steps:

1. *Establish the fact of personal sin and the need for salvation* (Romans 3:9–20; 1 John 1:8; Luke 13:3, 5). Before a person can be saved, he must realize he is lost. [The remark has been made that if you had an hour to lead someone to the Lord, you should spend most of that hour convincing the person of his own sin and estrangement from God. Think of the woman at the well. She was somewhat interested in the living water, but her interest was not complete until Jesus made her aware of her own soul's thirst.]

2. *Explain the remedy that God and His Son Jesus Christ have provided* (John 3:14–21; Romans 4:22–5:1; Ephesians 2:8, 9). A brief but comprehensive review of Jesus' life would be beneficial at this point.

Chapter 4

3. *Explain the need of responding to God's provision.* There are many parts to man's response, and a thorough understanding is essential. Here again a look at many different Bible verses that give man's part will set the stage for a response.

A genuine response to God's provision includes (a) true repentance, which means to make a complete turn around with one's life—Acts 2:38; Luke 15:10; (b) receiving Christ and . . . exercising faith [in Him]—John 3:16; Romans 5:1; (c) confession of personal sin and the need to declare one's belief in Christ publicly—1 John 1:9; James 5:16; Romans 10:9, 10; Luke 9:26; (d) humbling oneself as a little child, which implies teachableness and openness to truth; . . . (e) the need for baptism—Acts 2:38; and (f) cross bearing—Luke 14:27.

Be ready to thoroughly explain all the big words you use. Many who do not know Christ have no idea of the meaning of words like *justification* or *sanctification*.

Why not take these steps and references and copy them on the blank pages of your Bible? Although you will never be able to save anyone by knowing what verses to read, you may be able to lead a soul to the point where Christ can save him.

Do not only know the plan and the verses but also put them to work. You may first . . . practice sharing them with a Christian friend. Then share these steps with someone who is unsaved. Say, "Would you know what to do if you ever did want to get right with God?" Or, "Has anyone ever explained to you God's plan of salvation?" Sometimes people are more anxious to hear if they know you are not planning to press them for a decision. Later you can check with them and discover if they have any questions, or are ready to make a decision for Christ.

When a person finally agrees that he would like to yield his life to God, ask him to turn to God in prayer. Say something like this, "I can't save you, and God won't save you for my sake. That's something you have to work out with God." Ask him to kneel down and tell God what he knows because of what you have taught him from the Bible. He will want to confess his sinfulness, ask for forgiveness, express his faith in Jesus, and ask Jesus into his heart.[14]

Leading people on with the Lord. People must understand that their covenant with the Lord will not maintain itself. They must keep it up. This involves several basic things:

(1) Worshiping the Lord personally, one to one. This involves prayer and Bible reading.

(2) Identifying publicly with the Lord. A Christian's appearance, language, and interests will set him apart from the crowd. So will the word he sometimes says for the Lord.

(3) Associating and worshiping with other Christians.

(4) Letting the Lord control his plans and sharpen his concepts of right and wrong and of what it means to be a follower of Christ.

---

[14] Stephen Ebersole, "Leading a Soul to Christ," *The Eastern Mennonite Testimony,* December 1987, p. 16, p. 7, adapted.

Chapter 5

Taking a Stand on Issues

The first families who arrive at a new outreach set the standards of lifestyle and personal appearance for the congregation. Of course, the sending church has already defined those standards, but the new little flock can support them or erode them by their own example. A sobering thought, is it not? This is why the sending church leaders are so careful whom they send. And it is why personnel who first arrive should pay careful attention to the pattern they are helping to establish.

Upholding the Standards

"Now I praise you, brethren, that ye remember me in all things, and keep the ordinances, as I delivered them to you."

1 Corinthians 11:2

Allaying our own fears. Outreach workers often struggle with the fear that by holding high standards they will lose people they are trying to reach. No one disputes the fact that sometimes they do. Even the ones who stay in the church can have some real struggles with the standards. One brother remarked that the first time he wore a plain coat, it took him three tries to get out the door.

Some propose that it is helpful to let down the bars a little. They recommend allowing more variety among people coming

CHAPTER 5

into the church. One brother argues that it is a very big step into Anabaptist culture; why should we make it even harder? Jesus did accuse the lawyers of His day, "Ye lade men with burdens grievous to be borne" (Luke 11:46). We do not want to be guilty of this by imposing capricious standards on people.

Some point out that certain church standards are unrealistic. It is hard to come up with a good illustration of this, however, even if we look at churches other than our own, for the standards we think ridiculous might have more sound reasoning behind them than we think. It is generally not the standards, but the corruption of the standards, that creates the real problem.

The word *legalism* also raises concern. Although legalism is a bit hard to define and apply, no one doubts that there is such a thing, and no one wants to be guilty of it.

There are a few other considerations, however.

We cannot please everyone. No matter where we draw our lines, we will attract some people and repel others. If we loosen our standards, we might no longer attract the kind of people we have been attracting. Remember also that some groups more conservative than our own are attracting people too.

For every newcomer who is troubled by our great degree of nonconformity, another is troubled by the lack of it. Such people do not ask, "Why are the women's head coverings so large?" but rather, "Why are they so small?" And "Why don't men wear their plain coats more often?" So conservatism in itself is not defeating our mission efforts.

Then too, we cannot avoid being somewhat arbitrary. Let us hasten to say that as much as possible we should *not* be arbitrary. We should base our standards on a "Thus saith the Lord." However, the Bible leaves many decisions up to the church to work out without specific direction.

Most newcomers to the church understand this, based on their own acquaintance with secular affairs. The majority of

Taking a Stand on Issues

states allow a young person to get a driver's license at age sixteen. People are sensible enough not to argue that age fifteen plus eleven months does not make much difference. They understand that somewhere, someone has to draw the line. Similarly, the church must say, "Here is a principle, and here is where we draw the line upholding that principle."

Practices not based directly on the Bible we should frankly acknowledge as such. However, some of those practices, such as twice-yearly Communion, have the support of many years. We should not rush to change things unless it becomes obvious that we should.

We should not fail to learn lessons from other churches. Certain churches that did let down the bars finally lost so much ground that they could hardly be recognized as the same church. Books have been written on this subject, of which the most vivid might be *Passing on the Faith*,[1] a history of Lancaster Mennonite High School and the church that supported it. Of course, passing on the faith was, in the end, what the school did not do.

By contrast, churches that stick to their own requirements not only save their people but hold people's respect. One man who was asked why he left one church for another replied in effect, "Our group preached it; yours practiced it." Another man who left a conservative congregation and then returned to it said, "The reason we left was your little book [the church discipline], and the reason we came back was your little book." Yet another man who tried a more liberal church declared when he returned, "I need fences and discipline."

We need to avoid experimentation. This does not mean we should freeze-dry everything our forefathers did and live strictly by it. Every generation must face new issues, make new decisions, and move forward into uncharted territory, whether

---

[1] Donald B. Kraybill, *Passing on the Faith: The Story of a Mennonite School*, (Intercourse, Pa.: Good Books).

Chapter 5

they like it or not. But we need to avoid the spirit described in Jeremiah 2:36: "Why gaddest thou about so much to change thy way?" One brother summed up the matter of experimentation succinctly: "By the time you find out it doesn't work, it will be too late to do anything about it."

Finally, what is the most important consideration? Is it not that our practices and standards are and ought to be an expression of our faith? We dare not speak of our practices mechanically, as if we were differentiating between shades of gray in a paint store. We do what we do out of a heart of love for the Lord.

When people leave the church, it does shake us up. Naturally, we search our souls and wonder what we did wrong. One answer is, "Not necessarily anything." In fact, they might have left because we did things *right*. The apostle John calmly wrote about the people who left his church: "They went out from us, but they were not of us; for if they had been of us, they would no doubt have continued with us: but they went out, that they might be made manifest that they were not all of us" (1 John 2:19).

What then might we be blamed for if people leave the church? Perhaps the most frequent reason people leave a church is not over standards at all, although the standards might be blamed. The problem might be social, with members wondering if they really are accepted in the church. It might be cultural, and it might be spiritual. It might be lack of unity in the church.

It might be that the standards were not explained clearly enough except for a weak "That's the way we've always done it." Then too it might be that members with little sympathy for the standards have corrupted them until they do not make sense to sensible people. (Have you not seen how a cape dress or veiling can be designed in a way that their purposes are defeated?) We need to lay the finger of blame on the problem that actually exists and let the Lord work on that.

Standards for the seekers. As people move toward joining our church, they make changes. They dress more conservatively, for one thing. Most of these changes we welcome. When we see other changes, we wonder if they are a bit premature.

Take, for example, one girl who began wearing a standard Mennonite head covering to worship services but had not yet quit wearing shorts during the week. Of course, this cheapened her Sunday practice considerably. Perhaps she does not yet understand all the practical aspects of discipleship. She needs to be helped to understand what a life consistent with the head covering means. If it is determined that true commitment is lacking, she should be encouraged either to make a commitment or to stop wearing the veiling for the time being.

It gets a little complicated when a girl wearing a scarf-type veiling comes to school. Does she represent a threat to what the school is trying to do? Will other girls want to imitate her?

The answer might vary from place to place. In one school, when the parents of a new student who wore a scarf-type veiling met with the school board, someone on the board simply asked, "What would you do if your daughter came home and said, 'I want to wear a covering like the ones the other girls wear'?" The parents replied, "She already talked about that." There was no struggle. In this case, the relaxed approach paid off.

A wife is less responsible for undesirable circumstances in the home than a husband is. However, she has some influence. One sister was so troubled by the television in her home that her husband finally moved it to a more private spot. At least it was a step in the right direction.

On nebulous matters like these, there may be a place for some tolerance for a time, especially considering the great distance some individuals have already come to join God's people. Because situations vary so much and opinions vary so much, it would be unwise to write prescriptions in this book. These questions need to be worked out among leaders who know the Lord and understand the situation.

CHAPTER 5

Relating to Other Church Groups
"Speak not evil one of another, brethren."
James 4:11

Conservative groups. How should we relate to other, more-or-less-conservative groups whose standards are somewhat different from our own? Very cautiously. "Good fences make good neighbors." It is probably better to have one fence too many than one fence too few.

However, while we need not endorse the work of other groups, neither should we try to undermine their work. "And John answered and said, Master, we saw one casting out devils in thy name; and we forbad him, because he followeth not with us. And Jesus said unto him, Forbid him not: for he that is not against us is for us" (Luke 9:49, 50).

To an extent we carry this principle even to church groups that have little in common with us. "Notwithstanding, every way, whether in pretence, or in truth, Christ is preached; and I therein do rejoice, yea, and will rejoice" (Philippians 1:18).

Local churches. Sometimes, of course, we must draw clear lines. A community pastor might call you and invite you to a prayer breakfast with a group of Protestant preachers in town. When you decline, he might say, "Aren't we all working together?"

People assume that if we work together, we work better. In many kinds of projects, that is true. However, on the community religious level, the opposite may be true. By standing aloof from other churches, we might challenge them more effectively to a closer walk with God than if we linked arms with them.

What about community programs? Shall we contribute to the cerebral palsy organization when they ask for anything used that we can set out on the front porch? What about the United Way representative who stands on the doorstep and wants money?

These people usually are not interested in a long explanation about how generous you are to your own church programs and why you have reservations about contributing to theirs. One telephone caller summed it up, "All we need is a yes or a no. A yes is great; a no is good." Keep any explanations short and concise. In some cases (e.g., a local community improvement), a moderate-sized donation would not be wrong, and it would keep up good relationships with local people.

Divorce and Remarriage

"And there shall in no wise enter into it any thing that defileth."
Revelation 21:27

"The Lord led us together," said a divorced man in his second marriage. He was typical of many divorced and remarried couples. Virtually every congregation reaching out to people will face situations like his.

It is painful to address two people who have established a happy home together and to point out that God does not approve of their marriage. We who live in a society that flees pain as much as possible can hardly believe that the Bible provides no "out" but to end the relationship, though many people have turned its pages over and over, trying to find one.

Interestingly, many people who find themselves involved in adultery respect the position of our church. One man who found himself in a wrong marriage thought the church should give him some consideration, since he had been unaware of all that the Bible teaches when he had married. Finally, someone asked the man, "Do you think the church should make an exception for you?" The man promptly replied, "No. You are what you are because of the stand you have taken. Furthermore, if you made an exception for me, you would end up making exceptions for many other people too."

One comfort we have about the pain involved is knowing that God gives grace to people for what He asks them to do.

Chapter 5

It is not perfectly accurate to compare the pain of couples who are separating with the pain we would feel if we would separate from our spouses. Since we have not needed the grace to take such a step, God has not given it to us, but He will see His children through in these situations. It will be hard, but it will be possible.

When people in impure marriages decide to live separately, should they move suddenly or gradually? That might vary, but they need to move rapidly enough to keep up their momentum. A vision allowed to fade can be very hard to restore.

There may be differences too in how couples should relate to each other after they separate. For example, if they have children to whom they are both responsible, this may call for more communication between them than if they had none. However, the most important consideration must be their personal Christian victory. "If thy right hand offend thee, cut it off" (Matthew 5:30). If an arrangement intended to work for everyone's good leads to temptation or frustration instead, then some other, safer arrangement must be made. The local ministry should be knowledgeable of questions people like this are facing and should give direction. Nothing must compromise the goal that Christ will someday present them faultless before the presence of His Father's glory with exceeding joy.

Finally, it is not enough merely to tell people what they may not do. If we expect them to sacrifice family life and social ties, then we as a church need to supply family and social life for them. The high casualty rate of those couples who have tried living apart from each other for conscience' sake speaks for itself. By meeting their needs, we are helping to fulfill Christ's promise, "There is no man that hath left house, or parents, or brethren, or wife, or children, for the kingdom of God's sake, who shall not receive manifold more in this present time, and in the world to come life everlasting" (Luke 18:29, 30).

Taking a Stand on Issues

Other Issues

"I speak as to wise men; judge ye what I say."
1 Corinthians 10:15

People ask questions of us that sometimes make us feel put on the spot. If we answer frankly, acknowledging the other side if there is any and admitting we do not know it all, the questioners will generally accept our answers. If we appear evasive or ingratiating, we will lose people's trust. The following questions deserve some comment.

"Why do you baptize the way you do?" The questioner has been immersed. He wonders why you have not been. What do you say?

Here are some interesting comments from articles about the mode of baptism that do not answer all possible questions but show the right spirit.

> The Mennonite Church was careful not to overemphasize the mode of baptism. Nearly all immersionist groups rebaptized by immersion those who had previously been baptized by pouring. The Mennonites, however, have not generally required one who has been immersed to be rebaptized by pouring. This is in harmony with the historic Mennonite belief that the immersionists were overemphasizing the mode of baptism nearly or altogether to the point of believing in baptismal regeneration.[2]

And again:

> I am not interested in trying to change those denominations who have practiced immersion

---

[2] Glenn E. Auker, "The Mode of Baptism in Mennonite History," *The Historical Journal,* reprinted in *The Christian Contender,* September 1999, p. 6.

CHAPTER 5

for generations, nor do I advocate that we need to rebaptize those who come to us having had a believer's baptism in another mode. But there is no reason for us to feel intimidated by those who teach that our baptism by pouring is inferior or invalid.[3]

Some Russian Bibles say, "Baptized *in* water" rather than "Baptized *with* water." There is little point in debating Greek terms at first. Without criticizing the Russian version, one could simply mention that our English Bible uses a different term. Look at the question again if someone wants to join your church and has serious questions about baptism.

"Why do you braid your little girl's hair?" The Bible does say, "not with broided hair" (1 Timothy 2:9), and sometimes this is pointed out to us. A simple answer would be that most Mennonites perceive a difference between braiding hair to be fancy or braiding it to be simple. *Broided* in 1 Timothy 2:9 is braiding ribbons into the hair, which is braiding to be fancy.

Therefore braids do not violate the principle of this passage (if in fact the style of the braiding is simple and without ornamentation). Further, braids are practical.

Just remember that in the eyes of the world, braids are beautiful. In one community, Mennonites stopped braiding their girls' hair to avoid being offensive to people who had challenged them on the subject.

"Why do you have Communion so seldom?" The questioner is used to having Communion much more often.

One minister likes to refer such questioners to the passage that says, "Christ our passover is sacrificed for us" (1 Corinthians 5:7). How often did Old Testament Jews keep the Passover? Once a year. Since Communion points back to Christ much as

---

[3] Dale Yoder, "Baptism by Pouring," *The Christian Contender,* February 2000, p. 10.

Taking a Stand on Issues

the Passover pointed forward to Him, it would seem that observing Communion twice a year comes reasonably close to a good standard.

In all these matters we have to appeal to people's hearts and not just to their heads. "The natural man receiveth not the things of the Spirit of God: . . . because they are spiritually discerned" (1 Corinthians 2:14). Let us be "comparing spiritual things with spiritual," and encouraging others to do the same.

Chapter 6

Life at Home

Family Life and Outreach Work

"But if any provide not for his own, and specially for those of his own house, he hath denied the faith."

1 Timothy 5:8

Family life and outreach work need not be separated. There have been settings in which missionaries went to the field alone and their children went to boarding school. That plan did not work well. Some children grew up to resent a God who would separate them from their parents. The parents too suffered the loss of enrichment they could have had with their children around them. Besides this, the presence of children could have done much for the mission effort.

Outreach workers with children can tell you that sometimes children pave the way before them. People in the supermarket stop to admire the baby. The neighbor lady whom you finally meet says, "Yes, I know you. I watch your children go by on their bicycles, and they often wave. Nice children." The families you visit warm up fast because some of your children are the same age as some of theirs.

Visitors in your home observe how the children relate to you and to each other, and how you relate to them. This is highly educational. One woman said, "You can read all the books in the world, but until you see people do it, you really don't know

Chapter 6

how." Another woman had read Mennonite literature on how to relate to children and talk to them, but she lamented, "I don't know the tones!" As families later moved into her area, she observed, at least in a small way, how it was done.

It may be more difficult to find housing for large families, but in the end they will more than make up for the difficulty in what they do for the church.

Children must have their needs met if they live at an outreach just as they must if they live in an established church. Father and Mother must take time for them. The younger the child is, the more explicit attention he needs. Further, children need to have local friends. Pen pals three thousand miles away are fine, but children need stable friends at school too. That is one good reason to have several families move into a new area at the same time. Solid, settled family life and friendships serve as a basis on which young people form convictions.

Family life is so important that in one outlying congregation special efforts were made to keep it alive. They have only one or two Sunday evening services a month. They try to have ministers' meetings during daytime hours so that the ministers can spend time at home during the evening.

If young people cannot have their social needs met, their families might need to return to their home area for a time. This is one reason why families serving in foreign countries come back to North America periodically, or even indefinitely.

Company

"Whom if thou bring forward on their journey after a godly sort, thou shalt do well."

3 John 6

You might get overnight company every weekend for months, or you might not get much company at all. Lack of company might be a problem. When company arrives in a near

Life at Home

constant stream is when questions arise. The following observations may be helpful.

The situation is probably temporary. As the years go on and the number of local families increases, the company will not all come to the same few homes. There will be more families to bear the responsibility, so it will no longer be a burden.

Sometimes company is just what you need. Remember when company came just in time to help you start your balky tractor or to move your freezer?

It all comes out right in the end. Some company comes and goes, leaving you a warm "Thank you!" and no more. That is all right. Other company does so much work for you and gives you so much besides ("to help you a little with expenses") that you are almost embarrassed to accept it all.

You can do some work without insulting your company. When visitors come, you may finish washing your car, of course; and certain other tasks come along the same line. Depending on what you were going to do, you can say, "Maybe you can lend me a hand." Most visitors feel good about being able to help with your work.

If visitors want to visit a nearby tourist attraction, sometimes you can give them a map and some directions and let them go themselves.

It is all right to keep meals simple. The company might actually be relieved if you do.

Tips for Visitors

"He abode with them, and wrought."

Acts 18:3

Here is some advice *to* company, adapted from an article called "Visiting the Mission Field."

> A trip to foreign churches or distant churches in the States can be a spiritual benefit both to the

CHAPTER 6

visitor and to the visited. It expands one's love for faithful Christians living in other cultures and localities.

When you plan to visit the mission field, it is good to talk to the committee responsible for the area you plan to visit. Some missions have printed guidelines to help the visitor prepare for the trip, such as things to take along, special rules to observe, and other helps. Be sure to read the guidelines that pertain to the area you plan to visit.

Scheduling is important for the visit to be successful. You expect mission workers to make accommodations for you, and to do this, they must know who is coming. You may need to adjust your plans and desires to fit into the schedule and limitations of the field. Sometimes travel groups will need to be separated for accommodations to be adequate.

You may be able to combine your visit with some special service. Committees often look for people to take vehicles and supplies to the field. At times during mission personnel furloughs, there are empty houses and personnel needs that the mission committees would like to have filled.

The appearance of a visitor is very important. Visitors should be sharing a consistent testimony by a conservative dress style. Casual dress can distract from such a testimony and even bring unrest to a field where issues are being addressed. The practices of the visitor should represent the home church, and they should faithfully support practices of the mission.

Take work clothes along. You might be able to help a family where you stay or help on a special

Life at Home

mission project. Always be prepared to support the church services and the outreach efforts.

Special attractions are available in some areas. However, your hosts may not have time to go along to these places. Some attractions are not good for the Christian due to worldly exposure or poor stewardship. It is good to discuss the places you want to go with the local leadership.

Consider a gift for the workers or the homes where you must stay. Keep in mind the extra meal costs and possibly fuel costs. Gifts carried to foreign fields, however, can be subject to custom taxes. Consider the additional charges to see if some gifts are worth taking. (Note: Sometimes when gifts are mailed to those serving, the taxes make the gift cost them more than it is worth.)

Visitors to the field may hear discussions about some of the people's spiritual needs or material struggles. They should try not to ask too many questions about matters that do not pertain to them. Likewise, when they return home, they need to use discretion as to what they share with others.

One should consider the stewardship involved in making a visit to the field. When one has spiritual goals and desires to help with the church program, it can be money well invested.[1]

A few more comments:

Do not look too rich when visiting poverty-stricken areas. A camera might cost what a native earns in a month.

Bringing food can relieve the host family. Grocery bills can

---

[1] Adapted from Dana Ressler's "Visiting the Mission Field," *The Eastern Mennonite Testimony,* March 2000, p. 1C.

CHAPTER 6

double or triple for a family that entertains company. Besides, maybe they are too busy to have a garden, or did not have a garden last year because they moved.

Before you leave, clean up after yourself if you can. If you live in a guesthouse or trailer, ask if you may strip the beds, launder things, and so forth.

Foster Children

"And he brought up Hadassah, that is, Esther, his uncle's daughter: for she had neither father nor mother."

Esther 2:7

It is hard to know what to do about some of the needs we come upon. For instance, what do you do when you are trying to help a home that can barely sustain itself? Perhaps the father is gone and the mother is losing control of the family. Children run unsupervised, and the house is uncared for.

Sometimes the children can be placed in better homes. Many of us can name friends who grew up in foster homes and benefited immeasurably from it. Some of you readers have been foster children yourselves.

However, before the church moves too quickly to take children out of troubled homes, we must look at the other side of the coin. We are dealing with people, and it is not always a simple matter to move human beings from point A to point B, even if our calculations indicate that B is better. Home, be it ever so humble, is still home to these children. Most of them will not lightly walk away from it. Neither will a normal mother lightly give up her children.

There is an even more serious consideration. God designed each home to be a home, an institution not lightly to be torn apart. A mother's instincts definitely underline God's original intent.

Life at Home

Even the courts of the land seem to sense these concerns and are reluctant to take children out of homes except under the most compelling circumstances. As a rule, rather than soliciting for children, we should let the parent or parents of the children contact us first. This not only shows respect for the home but also gives us some legal protection, since we are not a licensed state agency.

A middle-of-the-road approach might be to give the family in question as much hospitality in our homes as possible and to provide work for the children while allowing their home to remain a base as long as it is worthy of the name. A kind couple, who has proven to be discreet in what they pass on, might come into the home periodically to help organize.

What kind of homes shall take in the foster children?

The spiritual profile of such homes is easy enough: we need people who love the Lord and love children, who can provide for them both physically and spiritually.

The personality profile is not quite so simple. Serious, conscientious people, valuable as they are, may or may not do well with foster children. What is needed is people who can draw firm lines without feeling threatened if something irregular happens.

Homes with a farm environment have advantages over homes that are more citified. On farms, it is more likely that children will have regular chores and can work along with the parents.

But then again, not all potential foster parents will have all the looked-for qualifications. How many "best" foster parents can we have? We have to accept people with a heart for the work even if they have some "flat spots." After all, most of us grew up in homes that were less than perfect too.

Taking in foster children is not for the faint-hearted. We do not like to speak of "risk" when we are doing the Lord's work. But we might as well face it: many foster children have

Chapter 6

gone back into the world. There has been much heartache. Probably the younger the child, the more likely it is that foster parents can help him.

All we can say is, the work of caring for foster children goes on. No one who sees the successes is talking about quitting just because of some failures. Remember too that through this work some valuable contacts have been made. It is not just the children who have benefited, but their parents have too.

Following are some suggestions drawn up by a child-care committee.

GUIDELINES FOR FOSTER HOME CARE

1. Accept the child as one of your own. Foster children find their security by receiving loving care with firm control. Avoid the "special child" image that leads to unwholesome "special" treatment of the child.

2. Be sure the child understands the home standards and regulations. When violations occur, be sure the problem is not a matter of misunderstanding.

3. Apply corporal punishment when needed with discretion. Use an appropriate instrument applied only at the proper place. Do not strike arms, face, and so forth.

4. Teach the child responsibility by assigning some chores that must be completed satisfactorily.

5. Lead the child into spiritual interests. Activities such as bedtime prayers, Bible reading, praying, and singing should be expected. Many times these activities are foreign to the child.

6. If the child is in school, work closely with

Life at Home

the teacher in evaluating conduct and academic progress.

7. Be alert to any unwholesome speech, habits, or conduct. Many of these children were exposed to TV and other forms of sinful perversion.

8. Be confidential with information shared by the committee. Sometimes people ask questions that should remain unanswered.

9. Do not at any time make unfavorable comments or reflections involving the natural parents.

10. Contact the committee immediately upon any serious illness or accident.

11. Keep the medical records up-to-date. For smaller children follow the schedule for required inoculations.

12. All correspondence to natural home and related persons shall be channeled through the committee. Correspondence to other friends should be monitored by the foster family.

13. If you are not available to be contacted at your home for more than a 24-hour period, please inform the committee of your plans.

A few more thoughts:

Perhaps you should avoid placing two or more children from the same home into the same foster home. Two children can encourage each other in the same vices they may have had in the home they came from. Placing them in homes that have some contact with each other may be a good idea.

Foster children may have come from undisciplined homes. They may need patient teaching in elementary things such as sitting at the table to eat. Exercise extra love, patience, and firmness to meet their needs.

Parting with a child, when the time comes, is a difficult part of the work but must be handled graciously.

CHAPTER 6

Homes for Young Adults

"Him that is weak in the faith receive ye."
Romans 14:1

Sometimes a person comes into our circles who needs a "home away from home" for a few months or years before he establishes a home of his own. Perhaps he has never yet lived in a godly home and needs to learn the rhythms of daily life in a home where God is honored. He has some growing up to do; he needs to do some thinking and some working on his weaknesses.

What can you do for him besides taking him in? Make sure he is not a spectator. Draw him into life's activities. Give him some privacy, certainly, but encourage him not to hole up too long in his room. If he comes home a little late for supper, see if you can wait until he arrives. If he does not show up in the living room for family devotions, send someone to remind him.

Pay enough personal attention to him. One young man whose spiritual life was going downhill admitted to his host that, when he had come, he had expected they would do more talking together. Shortly after this he left the home and went out into a life of sin.

Never approve if he takes the attitude, "No wonder I act the way I do, after all the problems I've had." That is heresy. Problems make one's temptations understandable; they do not make one's sins excusable.

Expect to take on some risk. One young man taken into a home found out where various Mennonites in the community lived and then stole from them on Sunday mornings while they were in church. (However, a high-risk boarder can usually be identified beforehand; the offender in this case already had a prison record.)

Remember too that young adults will generally not respond as well or as soon to a Christian atmosphere as a child will.

Life at Home

Some of them have already been scarred by substance abuse, immorality, exposure to vile literature and videos, and much more. Some have been victims of child abuse. Some are already single parents.

Despite these dark pictures, some young men and women respond very well to the genial homes that take them in. Some of our church builders today can point with gratitude to the time they learned more about practical Christian living in a friend's home.

Chapter 7

Life in the Congregation

Keeping Ties With the Home Church[1]

> *"Epaphras, who is one of you, a servant of Christ, saluteth you, always labouring fervently for you in prayers."*
>
> *Colossians 4:12*

Paul and Barnabas were far from being independent missionaries. Their home church at Antioch sent them out, and to Antioch they returned. "And when they were come, and had gathered the church together, they rehearsed all that God had done with them, and how he had opened the door of faith unto the Gentiles. And there they abode long time with the disciples" (Acts 14:27, 28). Authorized by Antioch, answerable to Antioch.

In contrast to Paul and Barnabas, many of today's outreach workers move to the field and stay there. However, the principle remains the same. Authorized by the church, answerable to the church.

Besides Scripture precedent, why do we expect outreach work to come under the umbrella of the church at home? Why should workers, though governing themselves in day-to-day ways, still look homeward frequently for their guiding light?

---

[1] Much of this section is based on a sermon by H. Lynn Martin, "Endeavoring to Keep Unity Amidst Church Expansion."

Chapter 7

Here are reasons why:

1. What is good for the church at home is good for the outreach church a thousand miles away from the sending church. We are all part of the same body, and that includes missions. In fact, some people even avoid the word *mission* in favor of the term *church extension.*

2. Being answerable to a home church helps leaders to think their steps through more carefully. When they must ask themselves, "How will this look to the church at home?" they will make fewer mistakes.

3. Being accountable to the church at home means more minds are available to help with perplexing issues. It may be true that leaders back home might not know all the details pertaining to a problem out on the field. However, it is equally true that they can probably look at the matter with greater objectivity than an outreach worker can who is deeply immersed in his problems.

4. Ties to home help to alleviate burnout. Much is expected from outreach workers—sometimes too much for comfort. But unity with a home church means that visitors will come, some on scheduled ministerial visits and some on their own. The outreach worker is refreshed by these contacts.

5. Unity with the home church gives more potential for outreach. There are more resources for finances and potential for personnel. Some mission efforts are limping along because they have a smaller support base.

6. Unity gives a sense of closeness and brotherhood. Letters and telephone calls assure you that the general brotherhood has an interest in what you are doing. So do visits back home. Outreach workers have testified, "It was an encouragement to go home and see the home people standing firm." They realized anew that they were not the only ones fighting the battle.

Now let us beware of some snares:

1. Beware of being impatient with the processes involved, or of intimidation by people who make fun of your having to

Life in the Congregation

"get permission from headquarters." The process of delay sometimes is an advantage in itself. Issues can become clearer or begin to resolve themselves during the time involved.

2. Beware of an independent spirit. When children resent having to answer to parents, it shows they are not ready to be independent. Outreach churches need brethren who say, "How do they do this back home?"

3. Beware of arguing, "It's so different here that the church at home can't understand." As was pointed out before, outreach workers can lose their own perspective and understanding. Friends back home can help to resupply this.

4. Beware of feeling closer to people on the field than to your brethren in the home church. One can become so good at identifying with the people he is trying to help that his identity with the home church suffers.

5. Beware of the test of time. At the time of this writing, most of our leaders at outreaches remember when they lived in the home churches. However, another generation is arising, some of whom always lived on the perimeter. This is good, but we have yet to see how well we can tie the churches together indefinitely. One answer might be always to keep at outreaches a few brethren who have moved from the home churches.

6. Beware the attitude that "the Spirit can speak to us just as well as to the people back home." How does the Spirit speak? Through the body collectively, in which saints from far and near share their insights.

Here, in conclusion, are a few cautions and suggestions:

1. Have a uniform standard, with members at outreaches observing the same practices that members do back home. (There will be reasonable exceptions, as with a member who never wore shoes in his life. In his case, the question of footwear color is unimportant.) A uniform standard protects the home church because it keeps loose standards from slipping in from the mission field. It protects members on the field too because

CHAPTER 7

it helps them feel tied in. We are all one, and we look like it.

2. Send only personnel who are committed conservatives, people who believe in conservatism from the heart and do not just conform because they have to. Send steady workers; adventuresome spirits are not always the most committed. Send common brethren and sisters, the nonprofessionals.

3. Keep up the travel contact. Young people, even if thousands of miles away, should travel to winter Bible school. Bishops must not lose touch with outlying areas. (Some programs keep two bishops from home relating to each work in a foreign country.) Foreign workers need to take furloughs, not so much because they need a rest as because they need to stay in touch.

4. All this travel makes up a significant part of the mission budget. Sometimes it is costly for missionaries too. (How would you like to take a furlough from your business for three months? Would it not suffer?) However, keeping up church unity is worth the cost.

5. Finally, keep calm in the face of tests. There will be disappointments, disagreements, and mistakes. The Lord is watching to see what we do with them. He will make sure the price tag is lower than the benefits and values of reaching out.

Relationships Within the Local Brotherhood

"Watch ye, stand fast in the faith, quit you like men, be strong."

1 Corinthians 16:13

A few years ago an outlying congregation was the scene of a strange paradox. Perhaps no other congregation in the church fellowship enjoyed so much outside interest while suffering from so much internal dissension. Naturally, the paradox did not last long. The dissension died down, but not before much of the outside interest had dwindled away. The congregation even lost some of its core families.

Life in the Congregation

What are we to learn from this?

Beware of an intelligent and crafty enemy. Satan wants to spoil things if he can, especially if he sees that people are slipping away from him. Sometimes he even finds disciples to serve his purposes. We do well to say, as the twelve said to Jesus, "Lord, is it I?"

Keep the vexations from destroying the appreciation. The people who exasperate us the most might be making a contribution no one else would make. For example, the family who does not "click" with us might have a gift for making contacts with the community.

Have an opinion without being opinionated. When someone contacts you for your opinion, a few stock expressions might help. "Well, my first reaction would be . . ." leaves the door open for you to change your mind. "Personally . . ." means you respect the opinions of other people too. However, offering no opinion at all (when in fact you have one) is a formula for trouble. Offer it, but do it graciously.

Avoid getting snagged on small issues. One brother remembers being taken aback at a funeral where the chorister was told to lead singing from the front. Never in his life had he seen funeral singing led like this, and it seemed strange and unnatural and—not right! Nevertheless, the funeral proceeded, and without great harm. Someone has appropriately said, "On matters of principle, stand like a rock. On matters of taste, swim with the current."

This applies to many other things. Suppose that for the big meetings, Sister Faye wants to keep the food list simple and basic, but Sister Angela wants to go to more work. It is not that important. Ask any man. Once someone experimentally asked a brother at an all-day meeting if he knew what he had had for lunch. His reply: "Food!"

One of the biggest snags for outreach workers is disagreeing on how to help people. Helping people is why they are

Chapter 7

there, and they might have strong feelings about it. Furthermore, the closer they are to the person they are trying to help, the harder it is to accept that other people have some say in how to help him.

It is good to remember at this point that the quantity of help we give people is not the critical thing. Rather it is the dependability of our help. We should not promise to transport someone's children to school if we cannot do it. On the other hand, if the school board promises to supply some family with a tutor half a day a week and the tutor does at least that much or more, a good relationship is built.

Do not make promises on behalf of other workers without their knowledge and consent. We have no business promising to open our school to a certain family if the school board has not authorized us to do so. Neither should we take it on ourselves to suggest to a family that the church will supply them with a place to live if they move into the community. If we put other workers on the spot, they might disappoint not only us but also the person to whom we made a rash promise.

Be as definite as you can with people. It might be all right simply to ignore someone's broad hint that he needs money. However, it can be better to say, "We do not see our way clear to give you money at this time." Similarly, if you do have a plan to help someone, let him know as soon as you can. People do not like to be kept in suspense.

Have a default mode. Who is sponsoring the outreach? Is it a particular church or bishop district? If the brethren at the outreach are "split down the middle," you will probably do it the way it is done in the sponsoring district.

Doing it another person's way is sometimes a matter of choice. If you are a trailblazer, drop to the rear sometimes and follow someone else's trail. This can be instructive and interesting.

Work toward system and predictability. The fruit basket gets upset often enough at first. It should happen less often as time

Life in the Congregation

goes by. Unless it cannot be helped, avoid coming up with an idea for switching things around at the last minute. Eager reorganizers (1) tend to distress members who thought they had already done their homework on the subject, and (2) often forget to figure all considerations into the equation—considerations that people had thought of earlier.

Do not fear strong personalities. Some people have definite ways of saying things but will back off graciously if someone points up the other side. If your relationship is ruled by fear, you will be tempted to make little jabbing remarks to deflate the other person. (For example, "I hear that Wilmer's saved two hundred dollars at the IGA. *What* did they buy?")

React to issues rather than to each other. It is true that a person's past record sheds light on his remarks today. But sometimes a listener focuses only on this and misses the fact that this time the person is saying something sensible. If your heart beats faster every time you shake hands with a certain someone, you will understandably have trouble hearing him for what he says instead of for what he is. However, do try to hear.

If you are corrected for some misdemeanor, try not to overreact. There is a two-year-old in all of us that wants to sulk in a corner when we have had our hands slapped. Let us rise above that temptation. Be slow to help someone regret a hasty word or deed, especially if what he did is not his habit. Most of our failures happen when we are taken off guard, and we regret them within twenty-four hours without any prompting. If that is true for us, we may assume it is true for others too.

Let the people most affected by a question have a hand in making a decision. When a question arose in one school about whether or not to have a program on the last day, the teachers were not enthusiastic. They had not been used to last-day programs, and one teacher was barely coping with the physical demands of everyday school life. So there was no school program. People who have the most at stake should not always have

Chapter 7

their way, but at least they should have a voice in the matter.

Think twice about having a minister work as a member's employee. Sometimes this arrangement works. On the other hand, it exposes the leader's flaws and makes him accountable to a man who is also accountable to him.

Avoid pooling your resources if it can be helped. A description of one such arrangement follows:

> Mission families divided the groceries brought home by others or banded together in one vehicle for business trips to town. They joined in butchering and dividing the meat. Sometimes the "mission family" took on double meaning when two families shared the same house. . . . We have learned that unnecessary stress is avoided by maintaining normal family life as much as possible.[2]

One problem with pooling resources is that someone is apt to take advantage of the others—or, more likely, is liable to be perceived as taking advantage of the others. This will create unpleasant feelings.

Remember that new members belong to the fellowship too. We should include them not only in order to help them "feel included" but also for the benefit of their insights. Even when we disagree with them, it might help us rethink and re-express what we believe and why.

Do not let differences in people's situations impress you. A class system can develop if some families are rich and some are poor. However, it does not need to work that way. Rather, each should appreciate the merits of the other's contribution, and the differences in people should draw them together. "Let the brother of low degree rejoice in that he is exalted: but the rich, in that he is made low" (James 1:9, 10).

---

[2] Larry Weaver family, "Guatemala News: The Work in Retrospect," *The Eastern Mennonite Testimony,* May 1992, p. 8.

Life in the Congregation

Turn some practical decisions over to individuals and committees. This not only relieves the ministry but also avoids some dangers. There is nothing the enemy likes better than to see the ministry divide over relatively small issues.

If you are a leader with a forceful personality, avoid giving the appearance that you have made the church outreach your personal stronghold. After all, there is a school board, and there are Sunday school officers. Though leader, you are still a member of a team.

On the other hand, depending on your personality, you should be careful not to give the appearance that you are some member's puppet, especially if that member is your wife. (A leader's wife too should avoid the appearance of being partial to one member's advice.) In a small fellowship, perhaps people are a bit more sensitive about this, since each member makes up a rather large fraction of the congregation, and since it is easy to compare the amount of influence one member has with the amount some other member has.

However, enjoy your congregation for what it is, even if it is small. Small outreach churches are not necessarily handicapped socially. It is interesting that in the smaller congregations, the people often seem to stand around and talk longer after church than they do in the big ones. Maybe it is because they know each other better and have more in common.

Be patient with processes. You might think that after a year or two of acquaintance, you and your new friends understand each other. Do not be surprised if issues turn up that send you back to the drawing boards again.

Finally, manifest the fruit of the Spirit, rather than talking to others about your disappointments in people and evaluating the weaknesses of individuals. People coming in should see a major difference between the world and us so that they do not end up saying, "They're really not different from anyone else."

CHAPTER 7

Our Attitude Toward Incoming Mennonites[3]

"And Ananias went his way, and entered into the house; and putting his hands on him said, Brother Saul..."

Acts 9:17

When two streams meet, it takes awhile until they blend. When people from different cultures meet and try to blend, there will be some ripples and eddies.

It should not come as a surprise to us that we live in a different culture from the world around us; sometimes we do not think of it as a culture. The fact remains that our applications of Scripture have produced their own culture. There is a barrier between us and others that we do not see as well as they do. One woman introduced to Mennonite life said, "I feel as if I was dropped from an airplane into a new country."

Is it any wonder that they raise questions about which we have never thought? They might want to know, "Are we welcome to your services even if we are not members?" This question settled, they might ask, "How long can I attend until I have to join your church?" These are just the beginning questions. Besides answering questions, what can we do to surmount the cultural barrier?

Be friendly. First impressions count. Smile when meeting people, whether it is those who normally attend or the newcomer. Be warm and congenial when initiating the conversation after the service, especially with the visitor.

Children are especially sensitive to their welcome when they walk into a strange church. If it is Sunday morning, someone

---

[3] Much of this section is based on an address by Richard Mummau, "Relating to Those From Non-Mennonite Background," and Mummau, "Relating to New Members and Those Interested in Our Church," *The Christian Contender,* March 1997, pp. 6–10.

should direct or show them to their Sunday school classes. After church, someone might want to point out to a local child that visitors are here and no doubt would be glad if someone would talk to them. You might want to give your tips in private. Formal introductions by adults sometimes tend to embarrass young people.

When we invite visitors home for lunch, is our hospitality spontaneous?

Be accepting. Those coming in among us sometimes perceive us as thinking we are above them. We should do all we can to help such feel accepted as they are, not requiring them to adjust to all our practices immediately.

Romans 14:1 says, "Him that is weak in the faith receive . . ." (take to oneself, welcome). Many who are coming into our churches have taken a stand for the Lord in settings where they have had to stand alone. They have lost their former friends and maybe even their relationships with relatives. We might not have been willing to go through what they did to get to where they are.

"Wherefore receive ye one another, as Christ also received us to the glory of God" (Romans 15:7). How did Christ receive you and me? He received us the way a father or mother receives a newborn baby. Parents of a newborn child accept the child as he is, even before the anticipated growth is obvious. Christ received us, understanding that every Christian begins differently from the way he will be after a time of growth.

Who is a Christian? 1 John 5:12 says it well: "He that hath the Son hath life." Anyone in whom the Son of God dwells is a Christian.

Although we should avoid calling just anyone a brother, we should assume a seeker is a Christian, rather than assuming he is not.

See the good in other groups. We cannot talk wrong about other groups and think right about our own. Other groups

Chapter 7

have given people help that turned their lives around. For example, they might have given someone a tape that was just what he needed at the point where he was. Many people have received help from places we would not have recommended that they go. "Whether in pretence, or in truth, Christ is preached; and I therein do rejoice, yea, and will rejoice" (Philippians 1:18).

Respect the head of the home. A husband does not lose his headship role if his wife joins the church and he does not. We will not help the home situation by bypassing the husband to talk to his wife, just because he is not a member and she is. However, there may be times when the husband openly opposes his wife's desire to serve the Lord and be a member of the church. In such cases, direct involvement with the wife will probably be necessary. Even then, she should be helped to respect her husband in every possible Scriptural way.

When the husband and wife are both members of the church, the ministry should go to the husband with their concerns about something the wife has done or is doing that they consider needs help. The Scriptures declare that a husband is the spiritual head of the home and that he is to dwell with his wife according to knowledge. (The word *knowledge* here refers to what he knows about her makeup, disposition, and abilities.) Generally, the husband will be able to accomplish more with his wife than anyone else can because he knows her best and has more insight into her personal struggles. When others interfere with the husband's role, the whole home can be disrupted.

The Bible order of headship is God, Christ, man, woman. This places the husband under the church and his wife under him, so when church or personal issues need to be addressed, the ministry should check with the husband before going to the wife. The husband may say, "I will take care of it." He may know that their involvement at that time would do more harm

Life in the Congregation

than good. The husband's decision needs to be honored.

Be patient. We relate each item in our culture to everything else we know; it just fits. But to newcomers, many things are foreign. When they come across an item, not being familiar with our culture, they may not comprehend. Understanding takes time.

Do not push too hard. When we see a little growth, we should be happy for it and not be too anxious to help it along. What we think is a little thing can be a major thing to them, and there might be involvements we know nothing about. When they have taken the step, they think they have really accomplished something. Let the step be as big to us as it is to them.

Let people make mistakes. When a brother from non-Mennonite background uses a slang word in telling a story, do not interrupt to say, "That's New York street language. Where did you learn that?" There might be a time to help a brother refine his terminology, but not in the middle of a story he is telling.

Be very slow to charge newcomers with rebellion or lack of submission. We may assume that newcomers understand what we are saying, when they do not understand. A fifty-year-old person who has been a Christian for five years may know less about the Scriptures than our own ten-year-old children who go to our schools. To judge one's motives and responses wrongly is to sin against him and against Christ, who died for him.

We show much mercy and patience while such ones are considering joining the church, telling them how much we appreciate them and their convictions. The same patience and mercy needs to continue after they join the church because there will still be much for them to learn. The Scriptures say, "Him that is weak in the faith receive ye, but not to doubtful disputations" (Romans 14:1).

Teach courtesy to children. When a stranger walks in late, he naturally feels odd if most of the children turn around and stare. The same principle applies after church. When children

Chapter 7

survey the visitor up and down, it is unnerving, or at least unpleasant. Invite such people into your home more often so your children get used to it.

Be courteous yourself. A woman urged her husband to come to church. However, he wore long pigtails in Indian tradition and said the people would laugh at him. His wife assured him they would not, so he tried it. She was right; the people were friendly, and no one said anything to him about his pigtails. He kept coming, and today he is a member.

Try not to put people on the spot. Suppose you get together for a meal. The host says, "Let's sing a verse or two of 'Where He May Lead Me I Will Go.' " It can make visitors feel uncomfortable if they do not know the song and sit there without anything to do until the song is over. Sing, "Jesus Loves Me," or "The Old Rugged Cross"—something that anyone knows. Our first duty is to put people in a state of happy ease. People should not feel on edge, wondering what is going to happen next.

About what do you talk? Gardening and canning? Talk about it only if you know that your visitor has an interest in and does gardening and canning.

Do not pry. If a person wants to talk about his past, it may be all right to ask questions. However, keep your antennae tuned to sense hesitancy or embarrassment on his part. Maybe you should back off and find something a little more neutral to talk about.

Another mistake is talking too long about relatives—who was cousin to whom. Yes, discovering a new tie between old friends is fun, like popping a piece into a jigsaw puzzle. However, the newcomer has no old friends or relatives, and all this is meaningless to him.

Try not to intimidate people by stating your preferences too definitely. There is nothing in the Bible about junk food. We avoid giving the impression by comments we make that we think avoiding junk food is a tenet of our faith.

Life in the Congregation

Avoid horn tooting. Do not talk up your church too much. Do not make your visiting friend feel that what they had before was nothing. The man who marries a widow and keeps talking about how much better a husband he is than her first husband will not get too far. Many people who join our church belonged to a fellowship before this and might still have friends there. They do not like the insinuation that by joining our church they went from zero to zenith.

Adopt someone. Mennonites allow some playing on a family level but draw the line on playing at bigger events. "Organized, contesting ball teams," for example, are out. Children play games with their cousins that they might not play at the school picnic. What, then, shall children from non-Mennonite families do? They have no cousins with whom to play.

Having an adoptive family is very necessary. If you compare the people who stayed in the church with those who left, often you will find that the difference hinged on whether or not the newcomers had someone they could share personal things with—someone who kept their confidences. Newcomers may often find someone other than the minister for their most personal friendships. They have often had to leave their cousins, uncles, and aunts behind. Share your relatives with them. Include them in family gatherings. It will fill a real need in their lives.

Respect others' convictions. Sometimes people have built strong convictions before coming to our church. What shall we ask them to do with those convictions if we see things differently? In some cases, we might ask them to reconsider their convictions if they want to join the church, lest what they are doing would cause unrest and confusion among the members. For example, a woman with a totally different style of head covering that she considers better than ours might cause younger sisters to wonder if they should adopt that style too. Assure them that adequate time will be given for adjustments.

Chapter 7

We should not treat other people's convictions lightly. If they lay their convictions down too quickly, they did not have strong convictions. If we ask them to violate their consciences, we are asking them to sin.

Churches working with people from Russian Mennonite background have allowed them to keep their children out of school to observe certain extrareligious holidays. Neither side made a great issue of it to the other; they just did things differently and got along fine.

Regularly teach and preach the doctrine of salvation by grace alone through faith. If newcomers hear this on a regular basis, they probably will be more ready to submit to our standards because they will understand that we are not basing our salvation on what we do.

When the ministry or anyone else decides to approach a newcomer about something in his Christian practice, it must be done in a way that will not bring discouragement, making the person feel like giving up. Working through and with a close friend of the newcomer can minimize misunderstandings and hard feelings. We should also be careful not to make an unnecessary fuss over him, but help him fit into the group as a whole.

Adjust your concept of mealtimes. You might wonder why certain friends never invite you for a meal. Well, having you for a meal might be a major undertaking; not every homemaker can throw a good meal onto the table at a minute's notice the way some can. If you sense that someone might like to have you for a meal but is hesitating, you could say, "How would it be if we would bring you some pizzas and share them with you?"

In contrast to this, certain cultures feel complimented when people just drop in—yes, for a meal! Their thinking is the opposite of many people's, but just as logical (within their own setting). Rather than inviting friends or waiting to be invited, they drop in on friends or wait to be dropped in on.

Life in the Congregation

Culture Shock[4]

"For he is our peace, who hath made both one, and hath broken down the middle wall of partition between us."

Ephesians 2:14

Mennonite culture may be thought of like an iceberg, with only a fraction of it showing above water. When someone comes into the church, he sees the 10 percent above the water, that which is obvious and observable. He sees the way people dress, the kind of food they eat, the way they talk, their sense of community (think of barn raisings), their peacefulness, their large families, their strong rural preferences, and their honest, hard work. He sees their church doctrines and their applications.

However, most of the culture lies below the surface to surprise the unwary newcomer. He has to bump into it and figure out what it means and how he must behave if he wants to fit into the new culture he is adopting. All these little things! This is the point where many newcomers become discouraged and give up. Following are some examples based on one brother's observations of the Mennonites he knew. Other conservative Mennonites would vary somewhat from this.

View of the church. Mennonites view coming into the church as if it were entering a kind of marriage. Leaving the denomination is like a divorce. Even leaving the congregation is a big move. If someone has had bad relationships in his home church, he must fix his fences there before he moves on to a new one. This puts a fair amount of pressure on restless people to conform to the church.

Worldly people do not have so high a view of the church. They do not care what you have done elsewhere, unless you are obviously troubled about it.

---

4 Much of this section is based on an interview with Tim Mooney.

Chapter 7

Mennonites respect the voice of the church and of the leaders in particular. Protestants think each person is responsible for his own relationship to the Lord. They do what they personally think is right.

Ministry. Conservative Mennonites do not go to seminaries, and they do not volunteer for the ministry. The church must ask them. Then they view the call as "a calling" and take it seriously.

However, in Protestant circles, if someone tells a friend, "I think I'd make a good bishop," his friend might reply, "Give it a try." A woman with this kind of background once confronted a Mennonite woman whose husband had been nominated for the ministry and said, "Why are you crying? It's an honor!"

Likewise, Mennonites do not generally volunteer for the mission field. Protestants pick a mission organization and go.

Protestants move their ministers around sometimes so that all can benefit from their personality and gifts. Mennonites call their men to minister to their home congregations, and that is where they stay until they are called elsewhere.

Frank talk. Mennonites tend to avoid mentioning names. When they do talk about unpleasant situations, they are indirect, almost hypothetical. People of the world give the name, the date, and the place.

Many Mennonites want to be inoffensive, so they communicate subtly, hoping to plant a seed in your mind and let it be your idea. Someone went to a new job and was told by his boss, "It would be nice if you would do so and so." Later the employer wondered why the worker was not doing it. Lo, it had been a command!

Another way of saying it: Mennonites put up a yield sign when they really want you to stop. Worldly people may not catch on to such hints; they are more blunt and expect people to be frank with them. When they air their views and others say nothing, they assume that silence gives consent. However,

Life in the Congregation

when Mennonites disagree, they tend to fall silent.

One newcomer into the fellowship made a move against which his friends tried to counsel him. He totally missed their warning flags and only later realized that he had blundered. His advice to "Golden Rule" Mennonites: "Use the golden two-by-four!"

Mennonites do not talk about how a difficult situation makes them feel. They do not say, "That really made me angry." They might say they were displeased or upset or disappointed. By contrast, a community man thinks it honest to say he was angry if he was.

Non-Mennonites are often frank about family problems. Mennonites prefer not to hang out the family's "dirty laundry." When newcomers discover that Mennonites are willing to listen to other people's family problems but not to share their own, they might perceive Mennonites as prying but secretive.

Non-Mennonites are often more frank about the facts of life than we are. This has to be handled graciously. If they start asking questions that make you uncomfortable, you could say, "I'll discuss that with you later after the children are outside." Remember that some people in today's society think nothing of having the family present in the room at a child's birth, so the difference between their way of thinking and ours can be a big gulf.

Employment. When Mennonites move, they keep in mind their proximity to a church fellowship. Church first, job second. The world puts the job first.

Fellow Mennonites care where you work. The world does not. So you want to teach in a public school? The world would say that is your own business. Mennonites will probably say it is not appropriate.

Male–female associations. In the world, a man whose car breaks down thinks nothing of taking a ride home with a woman. A Mennonite would rather suffer inconvenience. In fact, he

Chapter 7

would be careful how freely he even talks to a woman other than his wife. If he were doing repairs on a renter's house, he might take a child along with him so everything looks aboveboard. Married men take more care of their image than single men do. This concept is quite different from the world's, where married men are less careful—after all, they are married!

Family life. The family life of Mennonites may be hard to understand unless you stay with them for a while. Their image at home is considerably more relaxed than their public image. A man who looks puritanical at church and gives the impression he never laughs might laugh heartily at home and sometimes play with the children. He might even display some humor on the job. New members should not assume they must be very deadpan all the time. They should get to know their new brothers in a variety of situations in order not to get a distorted impression of what they should be.

Direction of travel. A Mennonite constantly asks himself, "Where will this lead?" He has seen how apostasy works all too often. A typical Protestant usually does not worry himself about such a question; in fact, it probably never occurs to him.

Lord's Day. Mennonites avoid talking about buying and selling on the Lord's Day. People outside Mennonite circles are often not that careful.

Formality. People in most communities think nothing of getting up Saturday morning and lounging around the house for a while in pajamas and robe. In the evening they might change into nightdress and then have a snack in the kitchen. Mennonites tend to dress the first thing in the morning and prepare for bed the last thing at night.

Animals. Quite a few Mennonites think animals belong outside the house—except for the fish and the parakeet, which they might not even have. They tend to take a commercial view of animals. A few even give the impression that they think animals are for shooting. Community people can find this very offensive.

Life in the Congregation

An analogy: moving into a foreign country. Moving into a new church is like moving into a new country. A foreigner in a strange land goes through several steps. First comes the romantic part, the honeymoon. Everything is new, different, and exciting.

Then culture shock hits. Familiar reference points are missing. A new resident finds himself dying to nearly all he once knew. He feels like a child among people who know their way around in social matters and in every other way. Sensing the overload on his emotions, a new resident begins to withdraw.

Next comes gradual acculturation. The new resident figures out the new norms. He likes it enough to keep going. It takes work. He seeks help.

Finally, the new resident reaches a permanent level of adjustment to the new culture. If he stabilizes at a negative point, he will leave. If he comes through with a positive state of mind, he will merge into the new culture. His children will never know what he went through. They grow up learning the language, the accent, everything.

Summary. These are difficult things to learn, and the new brother or sister must find his or her way through. Mennonites grow up with a culture that they would not grow up with if they were not Mennonites. Newcomers often have no way of learning these things until they hit a situation that teaches them, often suddenly and unpleasantly. They fumble to catch on. It is trial and error, and an error can be a real trial.

In light of this, someone should serve as cultural interpreter. When a bump takes place, someone should explain what just happened; otherwise, the newcomer might not figure it out.

If people leave the church after belonging for a few years, their problem was probably not church doctrine nor the church's application of it, but social difficulties, awkwardness, estrangement, isolation, and loneliness.

CHAPTER 7

The Needs of New Members

"Now our Lord . . . comfort your hearts, and stablish you in every good word and work."
2 Thessalonians 2:16, 17

The need for stability. Some new members are as solid and sensible as anyone you can find. Others never quite develop the stability that we, and they themselves, might wish. In fact, we should never assume that nonethnic Mennonites are the same in their thought patterns as people who grew up in the Mennonite church. Their children will feel natural as Mennonites because they are growing up in the church, but the parents themselves will always have their past. This does not mean there is anything wrong with them, but it might explain why struggles may surface in their minds years after they have joined the fellowship.

Sometimes the weakness of an individual member helps to strengthen the church. The other members learn Christian graces as they work along with him. They would not have this opportunity if all members were already "strong."

Then too a new convert might have some things to teach other members. Newly on fire for the Lord, perhaps he prays and testifies more effectively than many others. One mission worker wrote of a local Christian, "His zeal to fast put me to shame."

We speak sometimes of a new member's "simple faith." That is certainly no reason to be condescending. If only our faith were more simple! Sometimes they point out that we seem to be violating our own principles. We should not brush off their insights. Suppose, for example, that your children play "Sink the Battleship." It is all imaginary and seems innocent enough to you, but someone says, "I thought you were nonresistant!" Now we have learned something from him that is worthy of our consideration. Maybe you should look at the game again and consider modifying or getting rid of it.

Then too sometimes people are sensitive to their past. For

example, some people object to playing chess because they have come from a country where chess is a craze. We need to be respectful of concerns like these.

However, we must remember that in their zeal they might need to be steadied. For example, they might need some coaching on how to give their testimony to strangers without seeming pushy. They might appreciate help in sorting out what to make restitution for and where to find a place of rest.

In matters of dress, sometimes a new member will become much more conservative than the other members in the congregation, causing people to wonder about his motives. This has to be worked through. If no one helps him, he is liable to reach a point of desperation and leave the Mennonites.

Involuntarily the Mennonite leaders might contribute to this. Suppose a new member asks a question—about dress, for example—and puts the minister on the spot. To be on the safe side, the minister might give an extremely conservative answer that the church is not even practicing but that the new member dutifully tries to observe. After a while he sees that others are not doing it. This means requestioning and rethinking what the church really stands for and what the new member should reasonably be asked to do.

Some people's instability stems from the fact that they come from homes that left their needs unmet. They have the idea that there is a utopia out there. When they meet Mennonites, they think they have found it. The sooner they realize we have our problems too, the better.

And the sooner we face reality ourselves, the better. There might be too many stories in our literature in which the Christian (Mennonite) comes across with profound wisdom and someone else is impressed. What about the times when a person from the world is impressed at how *human* we are? That is important too.

The need for social life. It has been said that a courtship

CHAPTER 7

should continue past the wedding day through the years of marriage. A husband should always be giving his wife little attentions, and sometimes big ones. The same principle applies when new members come into the church.

For example, while we consider people to be visitors or seekers, we invite them into our homes quite frequently. After they become members, we tend to take them for granted. We might even expect them to entertain company of their own sometimes. They might not be ready for the change.

There are two ways to look at this. In the book *Cindy*, the main character made these remarks to her grandmother:

> "It's just like I told Ruth Miller the other day. At first I felt accepted. Everyone talked to me and made me feel like they were glad I was here. Now they do that less and less. I told Ruth I guess they are finding out where I came from—that I don't have a Christian background—so they don't welcome me so well any more.
>
> "But Ruth said, 'No, that is not the case. They accept you as well as they ever did. It is just that at first they put forth a special effort to make sure you knew that you were welcome and accepted. Now that you know that, they treat you just as they treat everyone else.' . . .
>
> "Ruth said I should feel good that I am treated just like the rest, because that means that I am truly accepted."[5]

This is perfectly true, and perhaps we should explain this to our incoming friends, as "Ruth" did to "Cindy." Still, a little extra attention to the relatively new comer has its place.

Then too, instruction meetings are over. The new members

---

[5] Margaret Anne Hooks, *Cindy* (Crockett, KY: Rod and Staff Publishers, 1984), pp. 305, 306.

could feel as if we have left them on their own—perhaps not a wrong perception! Since both they and we enjoyed instruction meeting, why not continue with something—say, once a month? A course on child training might be appropriate since some of our members are weak on that. Something about home economics might have a place.

Some feel special gatherings of people with non-Mennonite background might be helpful, filling the place of the family gatherings they no longer enjoy. However, reunions like this can serve to prolong new members' non-Mennonite identity and can drive a wedge between them and the church into which they are trying to fit.

New Members With Special Difficulties

"Warn them that are unruly, comfort the feebleminded, support the weak, be patient toward all men."

1 Thessalonians 5:14

Here are some personalities that might come into the church and that might need to be worked with. Naturally, people are much more complex than this, but these are presented "paper-doll fashion" for the sake of getting the point across.

The controller. Dirk came from a home that was often out of control. In later years, he would describe to friends how he saw his angry mother throwing at his father whatever was loose in the kitchen—anything from the frying pan to a full jar of peanut butter. Understandably, when Dirk became an adult, he wanted things under control.

However, someone like Dirk runs the danger of trying to take too much control into his own hands. Can he accept it if the teacher spanks his child? Can he work with the church leaders if they need to address needs in his family? Can he himself accept correction?

CHAPTER 7

Such a person may be helped if someone points out to him the damage that his topsy-turvy past has done to his outlook. Perhaps the church and school should give him a little extra consideration, always keeping communication open when decisions are made that pertain to his family. Finally, the church must not be intimidated. The whole brotherhood of believers must be considered, not just the problems of one person.

The independent one. Many parents who educate their children at home fall into this category. When society went for its merry slide, they shook their heads and stood off to the side. They would not send their children to public school or even the local "Christian" school for obvious reasons. They looked around for a church better than the ones they had known and thought they found it in ours.

There is one problem. The same independent spirit that enabled them to evaluate and reject society's mores now leads them to evaluate *our* mores. This is right and good, but there comes a point where a person must lay aside a few of his opinions in order to fit in with the group.

Fear enters the picture—the fear of losing the privilege to think. A person with such concerns must learn to imitate the wild geese. They think independently enough to leave the turkeys behind, but not so independently they cannot join the other geese. They fly wild, high, and free, but even then they fly in the shape of a V.

The apostle Paul put it well when he wrote to Philemon, "Without thy mind would I do nothing" (Philemon 14). Not that he ran to Philemon with all his decisions, but when he had to decide something that affected Philemon, he did consult with him. So must members do with the church.

There is a high price for noncompliance. A husband and wife who finally decide to go it alone without any church support risk emotional damage to themselves, not to mention risking the loss of their children, who grow up without any friends

Life in the Congregation

like themselves and finally throw away their parents' "funny notions."

The critic. This person has already gone through other churches, and now he comes to us. At first, he is very happy. "These people really preach Jesus Christ!" he says. Soon reality sets in. These people are common humans after all, and the perfect congregation is across another state line!

One critic went so far as to say the preaching had changed since she first listened to it. She had to be told, "The preaching hasn't changed. *You* have changed.'

Another critic agonized over the thought that many people in his congregation were not spiritual. But he himself was a poor example of spirituality, and that leads us to suspect that he was also a poor judge.

Another critic thought so ill of the people he went to church with that for a time he walked out shortly after the service was over.

None of the above critics is with the church they once attended, and if the church had followed them, it would have been torn three different directions. Again, we should learn what we can from our critics without being intimidated by them.

By the way, we should not be encouraging newcomers to criticize their former church to us.

The pedagogue. This newcomer not only criticizes our problems but also knows what we should do about them! He seems to think he understands us better than we understand ourselves. Occasionally that might be true, and then we must be honest enough to accept it. But remember, one of the pitfalls in outreach is listening too much to people coming into the church. There may come a time to ask, "Are you joining us, or are we joining you?"

The undisciplined. Some newcomers are unstable because they listen to their inner voice when they ought to be listening more to the voice of the church. They find it hard to submit to

Chapter 7

authority, probably because they are not used to it. Many such people are not used to schedules and discipline. They are not used to saving money. Some think the church owes them money, but they need to understand that self-denial is part of Christian victory.

These people excuse themselves with the idea that "you don't understand, because my background and circumstances are different from yours." In turn, we need to point out how much we have in common. We face the same enemy they do and have the same nature within. The church is full of people who have recognized these problems and have submitted to the church's direction as a way of dealing with them. Why should not the new member do the same?

By the way, now is the time for the new members to raise a generation more disciplined than they were. They can make their children sit still in church. At first, a few unusual incidents might take place. A child might wander up to the front of the church during a service because his mother thought it impossible to keep control of him. Yet after a little she will look around and see other people's children under control and decide she can do it too.

The family-affected member. One thing contributing to the instability of a member could be his family. Most of us can hardly imagine what it would be like to hold up Christ's banner in a home where no one else shares the same ideals. Yet, most of us could name friends who face this day after day.

The Bible does not give detailed instructions on what to do in these cases, only a simple ground rule. Jesus said, "Think not that I am come to send peace on earth: I came not to send peace, but a sword. For I am come to set a man at variance against his father, and the daughter against her mother, and the daughter in law against her mother in law. And a man's foes shall be they of his own household. He that loveth father or mother more than me is not worthy of me: and he that

Life in the Congregation

loveth son or daughter more than me is not worthy of me" (Matthew 10:34–37). When family competes with the Lord for loyalty, there should be no question who wins the contest. Once this basic principle is established, many questions fall into line without further ado.

That is why one congregation drew a firm line with a sister. Repeatedly, after she paid a lengthy visit to relatives, she had to confess that she had been drinking or watching television. Finally, the leaders told her she could no longer stay with relatives if she wanted to keep her membership.

Drawing a firm line actually makes some struggles easier. The same person who puzzles over which dress to wear does not struggle over whether or not to wear glasses, because that question has already been decided. And bumping up against a test of membership might be just the reassurance a member needs.

Besides being steady in discipline, what else can a church do? Mainly it is a matter of keeping in contact. Failing to do so can be a matter of lifetime regret. One brother remembers hearing of a member whose friends had left the church, and wonders why he did not make a simple telephone call before that member fell away too.

The church also has the right and duty to give direction, at least to point out what the Bible has to say. "Likewise, ye wives, be in subjection to your own husbands; that, if any obey not the word, they also may without the word be won by the conversation of the wives; while they behold your chaste conversation coupled with fear" (1 Peter 3:1, 2). The same principle applies to children. Ephesians 6:1 says, "Children, obey your parents in the Lord" (not "parents *who* are in the Lord," but "obey *in* the Lord.")

However, some ungodly family members harp on how a son or daughter should be obedient to them and dismiss the matter of obedience to God. Certain elders in Jerusalem tried to do the same thing, but Peter told them, "We ought to obey

Chapter 7

God rather than men" (Acts 5:29). As one church discipline puts it, "When the requirements of earthly authorities conflict with the requirements of Scriptures, we should unhesitatingly obey God."

This takes care of most of the questions. The remaining questions can be troublesome, however. In some instances, a person needs time to work through issues. "Sure, she's a Christian," one church leader said of a friend in a situation unsuitable for Christians. "She just needs to figure out how to do what she knows she has to do." Convictions, however, can fade if not soon acted upon.

Jesus Christ Himself did not try to answer all questions ahead of time. He told His disciples, "I have yet many things to say unto you, but ye cannot bear them now. Howbeit when he, the Spirit of truth, is come, he will guide you into all truth" (John 16:12, 13).

The illiterate are not necessarily unstable. But they do need extra consideration, as the following writer comments.

> In one case a husband and wife became members of the church, but neither of them could read or write. For a period of time, another church family living nearby invited this couple in for family devotions. This same family also helped this couple in studying their instruction class lessons.
>
> Another way of meeting their needs is to teach them to read and write. Recently the one brother schoolteacher was having reading and writing classes with two brethren who have families with children. One difficulty with this is that the family responsibilities result in a limited amount of time for study. . . .
>
> Another need that illiterate members have is to be able to feel useful in some way. Being illiterate does not mean that one is ignorant in

every way. Asking advice at times from illiterate members helps them to feel useful. Being involved in tract work and prison work helps to fill that need.

Sometimes because of the lack of understanding illiterate people may have, we may need to take time to explain problems or situations more clearly. We must be careful not to offend "one of these little ones." Such members may need additional help in material and financial responsibilities.[6]

The acceptance sponge. Some people who come to our churches have been rejected repeatedly. When they walk in at our door, they wonder if they are setting themselves up for some new rejection. They soak up all the acceptance they get and thirst for more. They also feel acutely any evidence of rejection, whether real or imagined. We who have gotten our acceptance in a steady stream over many years can hardly imagine how much acceptance these people need, or how long they might need extra reassurance.

What these people do not need from us is beatific, beaming faces but, rather, willingness to accept their contributions. Of course, as long as they are not members, there is a limit to how much we can use them. And even after they are members, their abilities still limit them somewhat, as is true of all members. Sometimes it is not the office we give them (trustee or secretary) or the contribution we ask them to make during church (having devotions), but rather little favors along the way. "Can you hold my baby for a moment?" "What's your opinion in this?" Sharing a problem in your life or a question you have always wondered about, rather than always shedding advice, might be balm to heal the soul.

---

[6] Lawrence H. Martin, "Relating to the Needs of Illiterate Members," *The Eastern Mennonite Testimony,* April 2001, p. 8.

CHAPTER 7

The moral struggler. Most of us have grown up in a sheltered environment. Although we struggle with the "old Adam," we have not been "dragged sideways through a fifty-mile swamp" the way some people have. We can hardly believe how it undoes a person when his mother was on drugs during the months before he was born, when his father sexually abused him, when the last nickel in the house went for alcohol, when holes were kicked in the wall and never repaired, when the TV was usually left blaring all night, when curses were the music of the home, and when his father finally left and never returned. For lack of better solace during his childhood, perhaps he became preoccupied with sordid things.

Now he comes to us, evidently as sincere as can be, but the old wounds run deep. On a normal day, he does well. However, when problems arise—he loses his job, his marriage becomes stressful, he has trouble sleeping—then the familiar demons touch his old weak spots and he hardly knows what to do.

How to counsel and direct him in detail (or, if he has fallen, how to help pick up the pieces) is beyond the scope of this book. There is literature on the subject, and we do well to acquaint ourselves with it. Certainly we know that "Christ is the answer" for every need, but do we know what the questions are, and do we know just how Christ answers those questions?

At times it can be hard to know whether an immoral person has really had a change of heart. If he has not, he might use religion as a cover-up. Two common indications of that are refusing to admit more of his problem than he has to and worrying more about the unpleasant results of his sin than about the sin itself.

Normal precautions only make sense. We should avoid leaving our children alone with people we do not absolutely trust. And as we would not allow our own children too much privacy when they play, we should not allow it when they play with other people's children.

Life in the Congregation

The single head of a household. In this age of broken homes, we may expect to minister to homes whose father is gone and whose mother is trying to raise the family. The handicaps of such a home can hardly be overstated. Yet the more closely we work with the family, the greater the possibility of success will be.

We cannot altogether fill the empty place left by the father, much less by the husband—nor should we try. A well-meaning brother trying too hard might fall into moral temptations he was not anticipating. Always he should involve his wife in his work with the family.

On the other hand, a single woman has no other adult to talk to in the home and will need to reach out—daily to other women and sometimes to kindly, affable men. This may help reduce her temptation to confide in her children too much and give them adult burdens too soon.

Boys from the home might be able to spend some after-school hours helping in brethren's farms or shops—not just for the sake of work but also for the interaction with a godly father. Families making social plans should take special interest in this family and invite them over (or invite themselves over) frequently. Think of ingenious excuses to get together. Make soft pretzels together, sing together, have family worship together. Probably one or two families will take the lead in this, but other families should do their part too.

Fractious children should learn that their mother does not stand alone in discipline. She represents all the fathers in the congregation! (In practical terms, however, only one or two will normally become directly involved.) A man might have to come in and administer corporal punishment at times. However, simply overseeing while the mother gives the spanking has several advantages. (1) The visiting father preserves the mystique of a power that the child has not yet reckoned with. (2) The mother preserves her right to administer punishment.

Chapter 7

(3) Potential legal problems might be less likely.

The mother might have problems of her own that she is struggling with or ought to be struggling with. They could involve her speech, her housekeeping, her driving habits, and, in general, her example to her own children. The sisters closest to her will want to give her some tips (ideas on scheduling, order, child training, voice control, and so on).

However, be gentle and patient. First things first. There is little point in rebuking her for the crumbs under the refrigerator while she is still giving nightly praise to her Maker for her victory over profanity. Remember too that expecting her to take charge of a home and yet always be as perfectly sweet as we are still trying to be is unrealistic.

Deal with little, practical problems before they get her down. Fixing her screen door is more important than fixing your own. At least you have an adult fellow sufferer, and she does not.

Respect all family members, including the absent father. Avoid terms like *deadbeat*. On the other hand, discussing the issues frankly with the children might have a place, even if it involves admitting where the father is wrong. Nothing is so huge and scary to a child as his own imagination about the unknown and unexplained.

Remember that although we feel weak, we can still "move the hand that moves the world." United prayer and fasting may have a place. God is watching. This family represents a great challenge—and greater potential than we dare to hope.

Our responsibility to newcomers. Although we are not responsible for weaknesses we see in new brethren and sisters, we are responsible not to cause undue difficulty for them. For example, one man remarked, "The first time I heard a child being spanked in church, I almost walked out." This does not mean the child was being spanked in the auditorium, but apparently the sound was heard. More discretion could have been in order.

Life in the Congregation

We are also responsible for the new brother or sister's finances, at least in part. Among some people, the rule seems to be "Especially unto them, which be of *my* own household." When a property is up for sale, they think of their brother in the flesh first, or tend to, rather than their new brother in the Lord. This does not communicate to the new brother that he is valued.

Identify with people's concerns—but not too much. Do you really want to view immorality the way an immoral person views it? Do you want to identify with all the grievances people have against the church? Seeing through other people's eyes can finally destroy you.

Finally, remember that the warmth of fellowship is what keeps us all in the brotherhood. Let us make sure everyone feels that genial warmth. And (this is addressed to the shy new member) try not to worry too much about how much warmth you are getting. Give it, and it will return to you. And if anyone ever says when he meets you, "Hmm, that's not a Mennonite name," it is perfectly right to retort with a smile, "It is now!"

Chapter 8

Some Thoughts in Closing

Losses
"He went away sorrowful."
Matthew 19:22

Losses in outreach are a fact. Losses of people hurt worse than any other kind. Someone analyzing his own congregation had this to say:

> A little review would tell us that there were thirty-four souls who had membership here at one time but no longer are with us. Three have married . . . and moved to other areas. Nineteen of these individuals are members or are seeking membership in other Anabaptist-related groups. One has gone on to eternity, one has gone back to nominal Christianity, and four are claiming to be spiritual but do not relate to any visible church body. But the saddest of all is that of the other six; three have become indifferent, and three have moved toward bitterness and appear to be turning their backs completely on Christ. Also many individuals have attended our worship services for an extended period, have even gone through the instruction classes, and in the end decided not to become members. Have we done all that

Chapter 8

we could or should have done?[1]

Many other congregations could write a similar report and ask a similar question.

The fault is not always ours. Jesus Himself suffered losses, as we see in John 6:66: "From that time many of his disciples went back, and walked no more with him." Jesus was not responsible for their choice. He was only responsible to confront them with that choice.

Neither should we assume that by holding the standard too high, we are to blame if people turn away. Jesus once set what appeared to be a cruelly high standard: "Sell whatsoever thou hast, and give to the poor, and thou shalt have treasure in heaven: and come, take up the cross, and follow me." When the young man who heard this turned away, Jesus did not blame Himself but said sadly, "How hardly shall they that have riches enter into the kingdom of God!" (Mark 10:21, 23).

We might as well say without apology, "Here is where we stand." What else can we do if some people leave us because we are too strict and others leave us because we are not strict enough? Can we not adjust to the desires of all the people who come? But what kind of church would we have by this time if we had been doing this? One advantage of staying at the same place is that if people ever want to come back, they know where to find us.

Despite all these reassurances, we hurt when people leave us. We wonder if we did something wrong.

Some fault may be ours. Maybe it is simply a matter of effort. At one outreach church, workers preparing for summer Bible school put up a tent, borrowed a bus, and invited community folks—and they came. Some of the children continued to come to Sunday school afterwards but soon lost interest. What was the reason? One brother suggested that it was the church people's

---

[1] Harry M. Erb, "Grays Prairie Mennonite Church History," *The Eastern Mennonite Testimony,* February 1998, p. 11.

Some Thoughts in Closing

fault; they did not try as hard to make Sunday school interesting as they had tried to make Bible school interesting. This was a point well taken.

Maybe we fail to stay in touch with people. Somehow, Mennonites keep up their friendship with each other even if they meet only two or three times a week. For other people, that might be a starvation diet. They may need telephone calls and drop-ins on a daily basis.

At one mission church where workers came from a distance, the time stretched long between Sunday services. After a woman gave up her church membership partway through the week, workers woke up to the fact that they needed to be present more often in order to encourage their members. It was then that they started having midweek prayer meetings. Their belated action came too late to save the sister who had already gone, but perhaps it saved some others.

Maybe we depend too much on momentum, assuming that, if someone has had a cheerful testimony for the past six months, he will always have it. Many struggles can simmer behind a smiling countenance. Leaving the door open for frank talk can help this.

Maybe some people simply get nudged off to the side too much. One young man came to church regularly for a year or two, and during that time he got invited out for a meal very few times—twice is a good guess. After a time he seemed to grow uneasy in church, attended fewer and fewer times, and finally left. He joined another church. Maybe he got more social life and encouragement there.

Maybe we pray too monotonously, naming our friend in prayer without saying, "Lord, what wilt thou have me to do?" Maybe we should have combined love with our praying and seen obvious ways we could have related to the person. One minister put it well when he said, "Where God is really working, we find that people are really working."

Chapter 8

Being too patient with people is as bad as not being patient enough. A lady named Carrie used to confess in tears the wrong things she had done but continued to scandalize her neighbors. The church bore with her at length—probably much too long—but in the end she lost out. Maybe if the church had dealt with her more briskly, she might have been saved or at least not been a poor advertisement for the church. The church lost a good testimony and lost Carrie too.

But then again, there was Maggie! She also confessed in tears sometimes. She would try, and try again, only to relapse. Or should we say she relapsed only to try again? If success is "rising one more time than you fall," Maggie illustrated this. When she died, she had a testimony of peace with God. A friend said after her death, "I believe Maggie went to heaven; I really do." So Carrie and Maggie finally went two different directions. We are back to the words "And of some have compassion, making a difference: and others save with fear, pulling them out of the fire" (Jude 22, 23).

Pushing a person forward too much can ruin him. Maybe one church did that when they first made contact with a group of foreign immigrants. They used a teenage boy to serve as interpreter for the speakers. After some months, the boy's general attitude became very negative. Had his self-image gotten too big for his actual size? No one can be sure what all went on in his mind and heart, but the church might do some things differently with him the second time—if there were a second time.

Some people move into the church too fast. One family did, against the gentle cautions of Mennonite friends. The mother in the family explained that if she did not move into the church fast, she might never move in at all. However, some time later she could not stand life in the church anymore and veered 180 degrees, opposing any members in the family who still wanted to belong to the church. Eventually the whole family lost out.

One brother suggests advising people, "Go to church with

Some Thoughts in Closing

the idea you're not going to join for a year." They need time to sort things out.

On many issues, it is better to wait to confront people until they ask questions. One woman who came out of an adulterous situation was glad the church did not at first come forward and tell her to separate from her husband. Had she done it out of obligation, she might have thought later, when difficulties arose because of the separation, that the separation had been a mistake. As it was, she chose out of inner conviction, and she had peace with her decision.

We have to consider people's backgrounds. One man was slow to join the church, partly because his background was from a church where people took their time to become members. Three or four years to join his church was not unheard of. His new church leaders were less perplexed about the man's slowness when they understood his frame of reference.

Maybe we are not frank enough. One minister says that in his past when people raised questions, he calculated his answers to give a good impression. He feels that people saw through this and got a bad impression instead.

Evangelism in reverse. Although Jesus was disappointed in the people who left Him, their leaving was part of a necessary process. He had to draw a hard line; it was His only way of sorting people out. However, the important question He raised was directed to the twelve: "Will ye also go away?"

Jesus did not want to lose the men He already had, men who were committed to serve Him. Later, as it developed, one man named Judas did desert Jesus, and that was a deep disappointment. The Bible says Jesus was "troubled in spirit" when He told His disciples, "One of you shall betray me" (John 13:21).

We who have already sold ourselves to the service of the Lord represent a great investment, not only from the Lord's people but also from the Lord Himself. Once in a while an outreach worker joins the very society he assayed to rescue

Chapter 8

other people from. This would seem to be a greater spiritual loss than someone walking away who never had much interest in the first place.

Sometimes workers have to be reminded of the potential for failure when someone leaves the church. No loss is so great that it could not become even greater if one more person loses out.

One way to keep this from happening is to avoid riding the emotional roller coaster with people. When someone goes down, the inexperienced worker might go down too, at great cost to his own well-being. After a time or two like this, no doubt most people learn to hold themselves a bit in reserve. A few workers have to be told.

Also, you will not rise and fall quite so sharply if you do things "as unto the Lord." You will be less likely to become proud if you succeed, and you will not go down as hard if you fail.

Speaking of leaving the church you have been a part of, leaving in itself might not be wrong. But do not forget what Russell Conwell said in his famous speech, *Acres of Diamonds:* "Of all the simpletons the stars shine on, I don't know of a worse one than the man who leaves one job before he has gotten another."[2] Might the same principle apply to leaving one's church as well?

Yes, frustration with the old church might run deep. But it only makes sense to preserve the old ties until you have a clear idea which direction you are going from here. The old adage about not jumping from the frying pan into the fire still holds considerable wisdom. By the way, you have your family to think of too. Perhaps you yourself can survive a period of fumbling and end up in a godly fellowship, but can your children?

After people have left, we can make another mistake by failing to communicate with them. If they do not hear from us for a while, they might think we have written them off. This

---

[2] Russel H. Conwell, *Acres of Diamonds* (Westwood, New Jersey: Fleming H. Revell Co., 1960), p. 16.

Some Thoughts in Closing

might be quite a startling realization to us if we have been assuming they are not interested in us because we have not heard from *them*.

In some cases people who leave us have not turned against the Lord, but have simply chosen another church. Naturally, we are disappointed to see them go, because we believe our own church is the best. (Otherwise, what are we doing in it?) Rather than panic at their going, we can remind them that our back door is still open. You never know. They might return.

Some do. One family showed an interest in a Mennonite fellowship but then patronized another church for a time. The Mennonites accepted this graciously. But when school time came, the family awoke to their need, not only for a school but also for a church. They began to attend much more faithfully.

In another case, a family did not show up at church for a while. A minister and his family went to visit them. During the conversation, he asked where they were going to church. "Sunnyside," the father said. "Our children like to go there." The minister asked the father if he liked the direction the church was going. The father said no. Then the minister asked, "Do you want your family to go that direction?" His point must have been well accepted because shortly afterwards the family began coming to church. As the years went on, most of their children married within the church and are solid church supporters today.

After one brother lost his membership in the church, he held a firm position against the church for years. Still, the church people kept a friendly contact with him. As his health deteriorated, something wakened him spiritually. The old barriers he had built up in his mind melted away. He got right with the Lord, renewed his friendship with the church, and was the old frank and open brother once more. For example, one time when the church leaders asked him to change something about his appearance, he said, "Why didn't you tell me sooner?" He held his membership with the church for several years and then

CHAPTER 8

died, giving a godly testimony to the end. All this did not happen without someone's prayers. The lesson for us: pray on!

Then too, a single brother became frustrated with the church and changed his membership to another. Still, he dropped in at the home church sometimes, and because he still held the same basic convictions and made himself at home at the old church, the members there treated him much like a brother. After some years, he returned.

Losses might in some cases be "false starts." There was Silver Lake. Workers tried for several years to win people to the Lord there, but it seemed the only thing they won was the ill will of the local taxi company. (The taxi did not like workers to take local people with them when they traveled to town.) Finally, the church moved to Stansfordsville, an hour's drive away.

Was the venture at Silver Lake a complete failure? Well, without Silver Lake, would there ever have been a work at Stansfordsville or at other congregations in the area? Then too, one girl at Silver Lake remembered her contact with Mennonites and after many years did finally find her way into the Mennonite church.

When God closes one door, He opens another.

Growth

"Of the increase of his government and peace there shall be no end."

Isaiah 9:7

Sometimes church growth is explosive; but more often it is slow, perhaps even discouragingly slow. What should we understand from this?

For one, the Holy Spirit moves in ways we do not understand. Who are we to measure our success? "Judge nothing before the time," Paul said in 1 Corinthians 4:5. We might be most successful in areas where we feel least successful and less

Some Thoughts in Closing

successful in areas where we thought we really shone. We should leave the measuring stick with the Lord and simply measure this: "Have I done today what I know I should have done?"

Secondly, how do we know success is not coming? In one case a new congregation opened in an outlying area, and the pioneers almost wondered why they had come. Hardly anyone from the community showed interest in their church. A few years later though, some did come, and explained that they had taken time to do a little observing first. They had liked what they saw, and here they were.

Thirdly, is the community fertile? Maybe not. The Spirit works best where people are most responsive. This is not because He lacks power, but because He will not sweep everyone before Him without their consent. Even the apostle Paul, effective missionary that he was, encountered unresponsive people at Athens, so he "departed from among them" (Acts 17:33). Yet even there a few responded.

When the church does grow rapidly, then what? Growth is cause for joy, not for glee. One of the biggest mistakes church people can make when they attract a following is to become too happy about it. Perhaps what they have is not growth, but simply community interest. Let them remember that people easily attracted can easily drift away again, as they did in the time of Jesus. They can slip away even faster if members at the core of the congregation have a wrong spirit.

What should be done? Humbly ask the Lord what to do next.

Instruction meetings. One thing to do is take applicants for membership through a series of instruction meetings, explaining the basics of the Christian life and church membership, and answering questions. This is no new idea at all. The early church fathers gave their applicants question-and-answer courses called catechisms.

Instruction meetings can be quite a pleasant time for a minister if he has a lively and alert group. They can ask some

CHAPTER 8

interesting questions! For example:

1. "If someone kept on wearing something that the church frowned on, would he be excommunicated right away?"
2. "My father is divorced and remarried. If he brings his wife to visit us, should we take him in?"
3. "I stole from a company that went bankrupt two years later. How do I make restitution, or shouldn't I?"
4. "How come some of your men wear buttons on their suit coat sleeves and some don't?"
5. "How do they figure out in church who's supposed to take his turn leading singing or talking or whatever?"

Instruction meetings not only satisfy people's questions but also help new Christians learn more about keeping their relationship with the Lord alive. Another way of saying it: they help them understand with the heart and not just with the head.

Instruction meetings are good for all of us. While we are trying to encourage other people in their growing, we find ourselves growing too.

Growing pains. Growth, at least at first, means that the members can feel overextended, trying to meet the needs of people who have so many, many needs. Which is better—to help many people a little or to help a few people more thoroughly? That is a question no one can answer with a sentence in a book, though it is worth pointing out that no church can supply a family with absolutely everything it needs. We live in an imperfect world, and God intends it to be that way.

Growth means new families in the church, with new influences. This tends to make some members uncomfortable, as they see people who are interested in the church doing the very things they have gotten away from. They wonder if they are safe in the church after all. Jealous for the purity of the church, sometimes they alert old church members to influences they would otherwise not have thought of. However, they also need to be patient with newcomers.

Some Thoughts in Closing

Growth eventually produces a different kind of church from what there was to start with. Members feel less responsible to each other. They feel less obliged to have company every Sunday. They know less about each other. These are not major problems, and some of them can be helped with a little attention and a little more effort to keep on reaching people.

Starting a new, new outreach. "And the things that thou hast heard of me among many witnesses, the same commit thou to faithful men, who shall be able to teach others also" (2 Timothy 2:2). Notice the march through the generations: Paul the writer . . . Timothy . . . "others also."

Growth finally means doing all over again what we once did at the "new outreach," which has now become an established church. Again, we must ask ourselves the old questions. Does the Lord actually want us to move into the new area we are considering? How do we know? Do we have the resources it takes? Is this really a Macedonian call? Who will lead the work, and who will help to staff it?

We might need to sacrifice family and friends, watching them go to the new outreach, as our family and friends once watched us go. Perhaps only then will we understand what our parents sacrificed one time. But God has rewards for us, just as He did for them.

Rewards

"I have no greater joy than to hear that my children walk in truth."

3 John 4

Growth means baptisms, weddings, and the satisfaction of seeing new homes start. Some of these new home builders may be our own sons and daughters. Others may be sons and daughters from homes that came into the faith since our outreach work began. The heads of some new homes—fascinating

Chapter 8

thought!—may be both. Growth could mean having grandchildren with names quite different from the standard "Mennonite names" we grew up with.

The rewards come too when we visit the weddings and funerals of community people. There we can compare the effects of the Gospel on some people with the sad plight of others. One man came back from such a gathering and said of his own church members, "The women looked like angels." By comparison, no doubt they did.

Growth means that our lives are enriched. We learn from the insights of others. For example, missionaries to Central America learn how to make do with simple things. They see people who are content with few of this world's goods, and they take up the challenge to view life that same way.

Growth means that although our children miss some things, they benefit more than they sacrifice. Children at an outreach church help to entertain more company; they travel more; they often see the eternal issues more clearly; they gain a wider vision of the work. Above all, they have the opportunity to gain a vision of the Lord that includes more aspects than if they had not been taught to reach out to people.

Some children live in quite a small world. They go to school, they visit their grandparents, and they feed the chickens. It is a nice world, but circumscribed. This is unfortunate. Whether in the home church or at the outreach, we should be reaching out to those who are seeking fellowship or to those who are lost. Maintaining the faith for ourselves is dependent in part on reaching out to others who have spiritual needs.

Working at a new outreach does involve effort and sacrifice. That is what life is all about. We sing, "According as her labors rise, / So her rewards increase." The Bible puts it this way in 2 Corinthians 9:6: "He which soweth sparingly shall reap also sparingly; and he which soweth bountifully shall reap also bountifully."

Useful Addresses

Rod and Staff Publishers Inc.
P.O. Box 3, Hwy. 172
Crockett, KY 41413-0003
Phone: 606-522-4348
Fax: 606-522-4896

Grace Press
2175 Division Hwy.
Ephrata, PA 17522
Phone: 717-354-0475
Fax: 717-355-0709

Lamp and Light Publishers
26 Road 5577
Farmington, NM 87401-1436
Phone: 505-632-3521
Fax: 505-632-1246

Eastern Mennonite Publications
40 Wood Corner Rd.
Ephrata, PA 17522
Phone: 717-733-7998
Fax: 717-733-2757

People Mentioned in This Book

Amendt, Henry, 18
Apollos, 24
Arturo, Don, 19
Baer, Mervin, 18
Barnabas, 133
Conwell, Russell, 174
Disciples (twelve), 26, 137, 162, 173
Elijah, 28
Elisha, 28
James (apostle), 28
John (apostle), 28, 112, 114
John the Baptist, 67
Jonah, 67
Judas, 173
Kingsley, Charles, 37
Lincoln, Abraham, 42
Lot in Sodom, 67
Mennonites in Russia, 20, 148
Mueller, George, 35
Nathanael, 27
Palmer, Ralph, 85
Paul (apostle), 13, 24, 30, 37, 102, 133, 158, 176, 177, 179
Penn, William, 26
Peter, 161
Philemon, 158
Russians, 16, 54
Solomon, 32
Steinhauer, Ivins, 13
Stephen, 103
Timothy, 179

Places Mentioned in This Book

Albany, Oregon, 80
Alturas, California, 51
Andros Island, Bahamas, 61
Antioch, 133
Athens, 177
Bahamas, 61–62
Boston, Massachusetts, 96
British Columbia, 17, 18, 64
Canada, 54, 59
California, 51
Central America, 180
Cheyenne, Wyoming, 18
Chuicabal, Guatemala, 19
Colorado, 18
Danskin, B.C., 18
Decker Lake, B.C., 18
Delaware, 18
El Edén, Guatemala, 19, 63
Farmington, New Mexico, 18
Fir Island, 91
Gap, Pennsylvania, 17
Georgia, 16
Guatemala, 19, 59
Highland, Delaware, 18
Jerusalem, 161

Loma, Colorado, 18
Massachusetts, 96
McBride, B.C., 18
Mendon, Massachusetts, 96
Nassau, Bahamas, 61
New Mexico, 18
Ontario, 96
Oregon, 80
Orwin, Pennsylvania, 46
Paraguay, 63
Pennsylvania, 17, 46, 91
Russia, 20, 54
Scranton, Pennsylvania, 17
Seattle, Washington, 91
Silver Lake, 176
Sodom, 67
Stansfordsville, 176
Tamaqua, Pennsylvania, 17
Texas, 16
Utah, 74
Vanderhoof, B.C., 17–18
Victoria, B.C., 64
West Virginia, 42
Wilkes-Barre, Pennsylvania, 17
Wilmington, Delaware, 18
Wyoming, 18

Bible References Used in This Book

Genesis 1:1 (11)
Genesis 19 (67)
Esther 2:7 (126)
Psalm 27:14 (97)
Proverbs 11:14 (32)
Proverbs 20:1 (86)
Ecclesiastes 9:10 (51)
Ecclesiastes 11:1 (79)
Isaiah 9:7 (176)
Isaiah 42:3 (99)
Jeremiah 1:8 (84)
Jeremiah 2:36 (112)
Daniel 7:9, 10 (11)
Jonah 3:4 (67)
Matthew 5:13 (54)
Matthew 5:30 (116)
Matthew 6:32 (43)
Matthew 8:20 (30)
Matthew 10:34–37 (161)
Matthew 12:1–5 (60)
Matthew 18:10 (51)
Matthew 19:22 (169)
Matthew 25:36 (83)
Matthew 26:22 (137)
Mark 1:4, 5 (67)
Mark 10:21, 23 (170)
Mark 14:8 (28)
Luke 9:26 (106)
Luke 9:49, 50 (114)
Luke 10:7 (39)

Luke 11:9 (77)
Luke 11:46 (110)
Luke 13:3, 5 (105)
Luke 14:27 (106)
Luke 15:10 (106)
Luke 17:2 (163)
Luke 18:29, 30 (116)
John 1:48 (27)
John 3:2, 3 (101)
John 3:14–21 (105)
John 3:16 (105, 106)
John 4:7 (97, 100)
John 4:24 (45)
John 4:38 (26)
John 6:66 (170)
John 6:67 (173)
John 8:12 (76)
John 10:10 (105)
John 13:21 (173)
John 16:12, 13 (162)
Acts 1:5 (118)
Acts 2:38 (106)
Acts 4:12 (96)
Acts 5:29 (161–162)
Acts 6:1 (43)
Acts 7 (103)
Acts 9:6 (171)
Acts 9:17 (142)
Acts 13:2 (15)
Acts 13:15 (102)

Acts 14:27, 28 (133)
Acts 15:22 (67)
Acts 16:13 (45)
Acts 17:23 (102)
Acts 17:33 (177)
Acts 18:3 (123)
Acts 20:24 (28)
Acts 20:34 (37)
Romans 3:9–20 (105)
Romans 4:22–5:1 (105)
Romans 5:1 (106)
Romans 10:9, 10 (106)
Romans 14:1 (130, 143, 145)
Romans 15:7 (143)
1 Corinthians 2:13 (119)
1 Corinthians 2:14 (119)
1 Corinthians 3:4 (24)
1 Corinthians 4:5 (176)
1 Corinthians 4:11 (30)
1 Corinthians 5:7 (118)
1 Corinthians 10:15 (117)
1 Corinthians 11:2 (109)
1 Corinthians 16:13 (136)
2 Corinthians 8:12 (35)
2 Corinthians 9:6 (180)
Galatians 6:5 (36)
Ephesians 2:8, 9 (105)
Ephesians 2:14 (149)
Ephesians 5:22 (174)
Ephesians 6:1 (161)
Philippians 1:18 (114, 144)
Philippians 4:2 (59)
Colossians 4:12 (133)
1 Thessalonians 2:19 (13)
1 Thessalonians 5:14 (157)
2 Thessalonians 2:16, 17 (154)
1 Timothy 2:9 (118)
1 Timothy 5:3, 4 (43)
1 Timothy 5:8 (121)
1 Timothy 5:22 (20)
2 Timothy 2:2 (179)
Titus 3:1 (59)
Philemon 14 (158)
Hebrews 11 (30)
Hebrews 11:37 (30)
James 1:9, 10 (140)
James 1:27 (43)
James 4:11 (114)
James 5:16 (106)
1 Peter 3:1, 2 (161)
1 Peter 3:15 (75)
1 John 1:8 (105)
1 John 1:9 (106)
1 John 2:19 (112)
1 John 3:17, 18 (43)
1 John 5:12 (143)
3 John 4 (179)
3 John 6 (122)
Jude 22, 23 (9, 172)
Revelation 21:4 (86)
Revelation 21:27 (115)

Index

acceptance, 143, 163
Acres of Diamonds, 174
addresses, 94, 181
administration, 25–26, 38, 50, 141
   school, 52, 57
advertising, 16, 68–69
animals, 103, 152
attitude toward incoming Mennonites, 142–148, 166–167
baptism, 106, 117–118, 179
Bible school, 70, 102, 136, 170–171
Bible studies, 16, 85, 92
books, 94–95
businesses, 51
children, 17, 21, 22, 27, 29, 31, 44–45, 48, 70, 81, 99, 102, 103–104, 116, 121–122, 135, 138, 142–143, 145, 145–146, 147, 154, 158–159, 161, 164, 165, 166, 180
Christian Contender, The, 142
church house, 15–16, 45–50
Cindy, 156
cities, 67, 95–96
committees, 25–26, 50, 71, 141
communication, 38, 150–151, 171, 173, 174
Communion, 111, 118–119
company, 122–123, 123–126, 134

conviction, 11, 147–148, 173
cottage meetings, 87–90
culture, 142, 145, 148, 149–153
   analogy, 153
curriculum, 51–52, 64, 72
difficulties of new members, 157–166
Dear Princess, 95
disaster aid, 91–92
discipleship, 107
distinctive doctrines, 72, 74
divorce and remarriage, 115–116, 173, 178
Eastern Mennonite Publications, 82
elderly people, 81, 88, 90, 98, 99
employment, 140, 150, 151
evangelism, 26, 27, 67–107
evangelism in reverse, 173–174
family life, 121–122, 147, 152
finances, 20, 21, 27, 35–43, 134, 138, 140, 163, 167
food, 48, 70, 137, 146, 148, 149
foster children/homes, 27, 126–129
Four Earthen Vessels, 96
frank talk, 150–151, 171, 173, 175
funerals, 96–97, 180
Gospel Herald, 28
Gospel signs, 85–87

Grace Press, 81
Guidelines for Foster Home Care, 128–129
Guidelines for Tract-Rack Evangelism, 75–79
head of the home, 144–145
  single, 39–42, 165–166
Herald Press, 96
home congregation, 20, 25, 31, 35, 36, 133–136, 150
homeschool conventions, 70–73
homeschooling, 18, 53, 58–59, 70–73, 82, 158
hospital visitation, 95, 97–98
housing, 21, 43–45, 122
incoming Mennonites,
  analogy, 142, 153
  attitude toward, 142–148
  culture shock, 149–153
  needs, 154–157
  responsibility toward, 142–148, 166–167
  special difficulties, 157–166
independence, 135, 158–159
instruction meetings, 169, 177–178
insurance, 62–63, 91–92
issues, 109–119, 134, 139, 141, 162
  baptism, 117–118
  braided hair, 118
  Communion, 118–119
  divorce and remarriage, 115–116
  relating to other church groups, 114–115
  standards, 109–113
jobs, 30, 51, 140, 150, 151
Lamp and Light Publishers, 81, 85
laws (legalities), 59–65, 127, 166
leaders, 15, 24–25, 25–26, 32, 122, 134, 140, 141, 144, 148, 150, 155, 177
leading people on with the Lord, 107
leading people to the Lord, 104–107
Licht des Lebens, 94
Light of Life, 93–94
literature, 69, 95
Living Waters, 82
local churches, 114–115
Luz de la vida, 94
methods of evangelism, 67–107
  advertising, 68–69
  Bible school, 70
  churchwide, 67–97
  cottage meetings, 87–90
  disaster aid, 91–92
  discipleship, 107
  Gospel signs, 85–87
  homeschool conventions, 70–73
  in cities, 95–96
  leading people to the Lord, 104–107
  monthly papers, 81–82
  newspaper interviews, 73–74
  other methods, 94–95
  periodicals, 92–94
  personal, 97–107

prison ministries, 83–85
public meetings, 67–70
recorded tapes, 82–83
retirement home programs, 81
scrapbooks, 87
street meetings, 74–75
summer Bible school, 70
through children, 103–104
tract racks, 75–81
tracts, 75–81, 104
visiting, 97–103
weddings and funerals, 96–97
ministry, 15, 24–25, 25–26, 32, 122, 134, 140, 141, 144, 148, 150, 155, 177
money, 20, 21, 27, 35–43
needs of new members, 154–157
   social life, 155–157
   stability, 154–155
newspaper interviews, 73–74
Passing on the Faith, 111
periodicals, 92–94
   Christian Contender, The, 142
   Licht des Lebens, 94
   Light of Life, 93–94
   Living Waters, 82
   Luz de la vida, 94
   Reaching Out, 94
   Star of Hope, 82
personnel, 19, 20–28, 134, 136
pets, 103, 152
prison ministries, 83–85
problems (difficulties), 16, 21, 130, 157–166

public meetings, 16, 67–70
Reaching Out, 94
reasons to stay
   poor, 28–30
   valid, 30–33
retirement-home programs, 81
Rod and Staff Publishers, 18, 26, 73, 75, 81, 82, 93, 94, 95
school, 48, 51–59, 64, 65, 138, 139, 180
   curriculum, 51–52, 64, 72
   from a distance, 53
   homeschool, 18, 53, 58–59, 70–73, 82, 158
   Mennonite-administrated schools, 54–58
   Mennonite schools, 58–59
   non-Mennonite schools, 54
   programs, 95, 139
schoolteachers, 52, 53, 54, 59, 64, 72, 139
Seattle Post-Intelligencer, 91
single heads of households, 39–42, 165–166
singles, 29, 30, 31, 82, 131
social needs, 122, 171
Sower Went Forth, A, 85
special difficulties of new members, 157–166
stability, 22, 154–155
standards, 109–113, 135–136, 170
Star of Hope, 82
street meetings, 74–75, 92
summer Bible school, 70, 170–171
tapes, 69, 72, 82–83, 95, 101

Time to Plant, A, 95
tract racks, 75–81
tracts, 72, 74–75, 75–81, 92, 101, 104
visitation, 90, 95, 97–103
visitors, 122–123, 123–126, 134
weddings and funerals, 96–97, 179, 180
welfare, 42–43
Ye Fathers, 95
Young Man, Be Strong, 95
youth/young people, 21, 31, 92, 111, 122, 130–131